Y0-BQE-592

90Λ

Managing the Economics of Owning, Leasing and Contracting Out Information Services

Managing the Economics of Owning, Leasing and Contracting Out Information Services

Anne Woodsworth
Long Island University

and

James F. Williams, II
University of Colorado at Boulder

Published by
Ashgate
Ashgate Publishing Limited
Gower House
Croft Road
Aldershot
Hants GU11 3HR
England

Ashgate Publishing Company
Old Post Road
Brookfield
Vermont 05036
USA

British Library and Library of Congress CIP data are available.

ISBN 1 85742 018 7

Typeset in 11 point Melior by Photoprint, Torquay, Devon and printed in Great Britain at the University Press, Cambridge.

This book is dedicated to our ardent
and devoted friendship and fellowship

Contents

List of Contributors

William Y. Arms
Harold Billings
John Black
Jane Burke
Carole Cotton
W. Michael Cowley
Robert B. Croneberger
Kenneth E. Dowlin
Malcolm Getz
Maurice Glicksman
Morris Goldstein
Robert M. Hayes
David A. Hoekema
Richard Rowe
Ward Shaw
K. Wayne Smith
Elsie M. Stephens
Lois M. Warren

Preface

Computing, information systems, and libraries are mysterious and marginal operations to most executives.

Mysterious in the sense that the fields mask their functions in jargon understood only by the initiated – the information scientists, chief information officers, librarians, or information resources managers; and

Marginal because libraries and information systems are part of operating overhead and not easily linked directly to profit-margins or organizational missions.

In the 1980s there was almost blind acceptance that information systems (IS) and information technology (IT) could give organizations a competitive edge. Now, information systems and services are viewed with a more jaundiced eye. They are still important, but are no longer seen as the panacea for falling profit lines or declining budget support (in the not-for-profit sector). Since technology has now permeated all aspects of business, manufacturing and service industries, executives are seeking ways to make more effective use of their investments and, of course, to spend less on information systems and related technologies if at all possible. Many organizations, including public institutions, are outsourcing computing services and other operations that do not involve their direct mission.

Operations like information resources and information technologies are thus a source of concern to executives, since a return on investments in IS and IT is not easy to see.

In the past, libraries have been conceptualized as being repositories of books, journals, technical reports, and other semi-permanently held materials, mostly in paper form. Computing systems were seen as lending support to the operational infrastructure of plants, businesses, and organizations. As the technologies improved during the 1970s and 1980s, information previously disseminated in paper form became available through electronic media. Computing and telecommunication systems broadened their functions to include rapid transmission of information and data. Computing systems and library information systems have now come to the point where they are heavily interdependent, if not functioning as one unit.

In recent years, executives have begun to outsource computing and telecommunications functions primarily to control costs. Traditional libraries and information centers have been disbanded in favor of service contracts or outright leasing of staff. Both the private and public sector are examining their information service operations from the point of view of cost-effectiveness. Decisions about owning versus leasing of information are being made daily. Decision-makers are finding that they must deal differently with funding and budgeting of information systems and libraries than they have in the past.

New paradigms for these service functions already exist. Not only have corporations and governments begun to contract out entire information service operations, but libraries themselves have begun to consider the costs, effectiveness, and implications of outsourcing some of their operations and services.

It has been accepted that service organizations differ from those with a profit motive. Even within the public service sector itself, the operations of service-like units that are merely supportive of the main mission of the organization are sometimes hard to understand. If understood, they are hard to break apart and analyze rationally from the point of view of having them make financial sense.

Thus, a tightening economy and technological trends have combined to raise anew some basic questions about leasing, contracting out, and/or outsourcing of information services. How, for example, should organizations define their 'core' information services? How can costs be controlled? Should we buy and keep information or should we contract for it as needed? Is there any value added when an information broker provides a service? Is it feasible to contract out a whole library operation as is done frequently with networks and computing services?

Our book provides a framework for decision-makers to view and review information services within their organizations. Entire units, components of libraries and information centers are defined and untangled so that the widest variety of organizations can analyze their own environments. While we have tried to minimize the use of library and computing jargon, a short glossary at the end of the work explains terms for which there is not a simple English language substitute. Each base chapter is accompanied by comments from a broad range of experts in the information field. Their comments enhance and enrich the perspectives in our book.

The first two chapters break apart and explain how information services and systems function within an organization and how this kind of work can be handled in-house or contracted out. The next two chapters describe the complexities of the information world – that is to say, the information resources and the technologies themselves. In each of these chapters, realistic advice is provided on issues such as cost-benefit analysis, the pros and cons of outsourcing, and other issues such as ownership versus pay-as-you-go procurement.

With collaborative ventures providing more opportunities for sharing of systems, services and resources, a chapter is devoted to the issues, problems and benefits of cooperative use of information systems and services. Then, prior to a review of future trends, there is a chapter devoted to fiscal issues – costing, pricing, internal charge-backs, and the dilemma of how to get 'hard' information about 'soft' services.

The tension in this work that results from differing values systems and beliefs are deeply rooted. For that reason we anticipate that portions of this book may engender strong reaction and counter-arguments from those who disagree with the models that we have proposed and would argue to be the future for successful information resource managers. We welcome this debate. The debate can only strengthen the role of information services providers within organizations and in society as a whole.

Acknowledgements

To the Senior Fellows of 1985 from UCLA's Graduate School of Library and Information Science we owe special thanks for their indefatigable support for the idea for this book and for their irrepressible suggestions about the issues that it ought to cover.

Nancy Allen, a 1987 UCLA Senior Fellow, Dean of Libraries at the University of Denver, kept us on track by asking the right ENTJ-type questions and reinforcing our ideas, particularly in the last two chapters. Our tireless secretaries (Mary Ann Caden at LIU and Patti Gassaway at UCB) ensured that all the pieces of paper got to all concerned and kept the fax machines humming. Sue McNaughton's faith in us, her continuing good cheer, flexibility, and astute observations served to nudge us into activity when our own energies and enthusiams flagged.

Finally, we must recognize the information technologies (IT) themselves, for allowing electronic communication and production of this work – from creation to cataloging of the finished product. Without IT, this book would not have existed.

Jim Williams
Anne Woodsworth
September 1992

1 Introduction

- ◆ Why worry about information?
- ◆ Defining information services
- ◆ Opposing views

« This book focuses upon a strong general trend in modern organizations towards 'outsourcing' specific functions. We are just beginning to understand the dynamics of this trend. Those functions which are most likely to be contracted out are ones that are highly specialized, involve substantial economies of scale, are relatively invisible to clients, and do not involve sensitive or proprietary knowledge. **»**

Richard Rowe

It is impossible to open a newspaper or magazine around the globe without seeing references to both tough economic times and our information society. The average person finds both equally difficult to understand. Both affect us all. From the perspective of information workers, the beginning of the 1990s heralded a dichotomous decade – one that provided unprecedented opportunities for innovation along with an identity crisis.

There is more information made available through more technological sources than most people can fathom. The information resources and delivery mechanisms that are now available have gone through decades of exponential growth, particularly in the past decade. The kinds of formats and the kinds of ways in which information can be obtained are now so complex and rich that experienced scholars and researchers encounter difficulties in their quest for information. Even information workers, trained to develop these information systems, often do not realize their full potential.

1

A company or organization with a small room full of technical reports often has difficulty keeping track of the information in them and wonders whether they ought to be computerized. Such an apparently easy and desirable solution can quickly become complicated. For example, how and with what technology will the printed texts be transferred into the computer? Who will decide which reports are out of date and discard those no longer needed? Who will provide the structured thesaurus of terms to be used? How will the work be done – by computers with near-human decision capacity? or by highly trained information professionals? Can the data input be done by existing staff or is it best done by an external contractor? Or is the information already in electronic form somewhere? If so, can a company buy a disk or tape or can the information be accessed as needed through computer-to-computer connections? If the choice is to make the text available through the company computer, what kinds of software are available that will allow it to be searched so that meaningful information is found when needed? Does the software require that information be entered in a pre-determined format? How much computer memory and time is the organization willing to commit to keep such information in-house? Would it be easier and cheaper to turn the whole collection over to an entrepreneurial information broker to manage? Does the organization have to reinvent the wheel in order to organize its information systems, services, and resources?

These questions and more are among those that must be answered when executives make decisions about their commitment to information systems and information services. Naisbitt and Aburdene (1990, p. xxiii) say that we will be forced to make decisions about many planetary concerns in the 1990s. We would argue that one of those planetary concerns will be the management of information resources at the global, organizational, and even the individual level.

The purpose of this book is to identify and describe the most important factors that must be considered in making decisions about the optimal ways to provide access to information – in short, the best way to use the humans, the machines, and the intangible resources known as information, particularly at the organizational level.

◆ Defining information services

Information services can most simply be described as a combination of information, technology, and people. For the purposes of this book, information services or information centers are defined as a set of activities that provide individuals with relatively easy access to data or information.

The information services centers most easily recognized are libraries. The medieval collection of manuscripts that was the center of mystery in *The Name of the Rose* was a kind of information center. The local school library that gives a ten-year-old student information about dinosaurs for a science project provides an information service. The Chemical Abstracts Service (CAS) that provides indexes to the contents of publications in the field of chemistry is an information service. The database of information that CAS builds, of articles, whole text, etc., is an information resource that is sold in various formats such as print, on computer tape, either to information services or directly to individuals through computer networks. The technologies and telecommunications that support libraries, the CAS operations and databases, and access to information resources are all commonly called information systems.

One way to try to understand information services is to analyze their common ingredients, which are:

1. Information professionals
2. Information resources
3. Delivery systems
4. Physical presence

This work deals only in passing with the physical environment in which information service centers operate. This is because the physical site and size of libraries and other information centers will assume less importance as electronic delivery of information increases.

Chapter 2 describes the operation of traditional information and library services and their current professional tenets. In this context it is important to note that information professionals in most traditional library settings are individuals who have a master's degree in library science. In Canada and the United States, employers usually require that the degree be from an accredited program. In the United Kingdom, librarians are normally required to be credentialed by the Library Association. There are, of course, other personnel who provide information services such as data entry operators, clericals, training specialists, subject experts, and computer and information science specialists.

The work done by regular full and part-time staff in a traditional information service operation is normally augmented by a limited amount of purchased outside services. These include contracts with consultants, who advise on the best ways to automate internal organizational operations, with subject experts who carry out special information retrieval and evaluation tasks under contract, with for-profit companies to perform entire functions. Some organizations, instead of relying on resident staff, contract for most if not all of their information services. Chapter 3 explores these options in detail.

Chapter 4 discusses buy and lease decisions from the perspective of information resources – namely kinds of 'containers' or formats in which information can be found, and options for finding and delivering it. When formats or 'containers' are mentioned in the context of a traditional library, books, magazines, and printed reports come easily to mind. Today, however, there are information containers that are less easily identifiable as such: laser disks, compact disks with digitally imprinted information, holographs, computer tapes, audio and video tapes and other forms of oral and visually recorded information. To provide access to information, computing and telecommunications infrastructures are used by information service centers to support the acquisition, organization and dissemination processes. Thus the hardware and software that enable access to and delivery of information *per se* are increasingly being considered to be part of an organization's information resource. Therefore, externally purchased resources most often include computing power, data network management, and access to databases of numeric, textual, or graphic information.

A large number of electronic databases exist that are for the most part maintained and owned by private enterprise. Access to these information resources is typically purchased on an as-needed basis. If, for example, a company engineer who is working on a better mouse-trap wants to determine if anyone else has patented one, his information professionals could search databases of patents and journal articles to see what others have done to date. In light of the number of databases, the choice of vendors from which to buy access, and the options of getting some or all of the same information in varying formats, the decision-making process about resources has become increasingly complex. Chapter 4 describes the kinds of information containers involved and their complexities insofar as costs and information are concerned.

The delivery systems that enable people to get the information they need for work, school, or recreational purposes is another key ingredient of information services and systems. Since time is a precious commodity for working adults, it is not surprising that the first recourse for information seekers is usually colleagues, not the closest library or information system. In the past, information seekers have not used traditional information centers as their first source. This is partly due to the fact that the points of access to information in traditional libraries have been limited largely to the telephone or in-person visits. Only for the home-bound or those living in remote areas has mail or direct delivery been a normal service. With a more information-conscious society, it is likely that there will be improvements in the methods of information delivery such as courier, electronic mail, telefacsimile transmission, and transfer of whole text (e.g. encyclopedias). With these kinds of improved delivery mechanisms, information seekers will find more avenues to use and more choices to make about where to get what they need.

The mechanisms for delivery – the computing and telecommunications services transfer of both requests and answers for information – have been under development for several decades. Their full potential has yet to be realized and the costs and ease of access have yet to rival the Eurail pass. With private sector information services exploring developments such as information kiosks in malls and book stores, everyday needs may be met more easily in the future. For the deeper and more esoteric information needs of scholars, researchers, engineers, and businesses, neither future information kiosks nor present-day public libraries can suffice. They will increasingly utilize a global computing and telecommunications infrastructure that delivers files and programs instantaneously. While researchers cannot as yet be 'beamed' physically to each other's laboratories, the capability exists for them to share information that underlies their collaborative research and to manipulate it as though they are actually working together in the same room. This capacity is now developing through cooperatively managed electronic network connections. These super-highways that span the globe now, such as the Internet, are fragile in many ways: financially, organizationally, and from a policy point of view. Governments around the world are putting in place the electronic communications capacities that will do for information transmission what the Autobahn in Germany and the Interstate highway system in the US did for commerce and travel. Chapters 6 and 7 explore these connections and how they will affect not just the delivery of information but also its costs. Someone pays for the super-highway systems. How their costs are spread, and whether or not cyclists and joggers can use them, are questions of the decade for information resources managers.

◆ Opposing views: to own or not to own

Another critical question to be asked about information services is whether or not it is best to own information resources. Before the advent of computing, the choice of buying books, reports, and information on paper or microfilm was clear-cut. There were no options. To be sure, organizations could and did rely on borrowing from one another but, for the most part, information service centers until recently have opted to buy and house information on the basis of what is often requested by their clients and what they anticipate will be needed by future users.

One of the identity crises facing information service centers is the identification of basic resources and services and what, if any, should be made available for a fee or purchased from outside contractors. There are few operations in any type of enterprise that are not locked into computer applications. Information services are no exception. For this reason, the opportunity exists for closer scrutiny of the use and cost of information resources as well as dramatic scaling back on retention of under-used resources and systems. Corporations do not hesitate to get rid of typewriters and computers that are collecting dust. If books, databases, and other information resources are not used, it may well be time to ask whether they should continue to be allowed to eat up overheads.

Buying information versus leasing access is looming as the question of the 21st century. In a society where free enterprise prevails, information is already being considered to be a highly saleable commodity. Once created, information does not need to disappear if it is sold, unless it is protected as being proprietary and confidential. Broadly speaking, the same information can be sold time and again. It can also be sold or disseminated in a variety of formats, such as print or electronic. From the perspective of organizations making choices about organizations' priorities, limited funding or space may force managers to make decisions about whether to rent, lease, or buy information as needed. If buying or leasing from outside contractors is an option, an organization might opt to contract for information delivery through either for-profit or non-profit collaborative enterprises. Shared processing and pooled information resources are sometimes used as vehicles to reduce costs. Even this less travelled route has pot-holes, however, as is pointed out in Chapter 6.

Issues of pricing information services, the debate about free versus fee based services are discussed in Chapter 7. It is relatively recently that information service operations have begun to recognize that they add value to the information that they store and deliver. In this chapter it is argued that more fullsome cost allocation is feasible, and perhaps even desirable, if information service centers in the non-profit sector are to remain viable and vital entities.

The confluence of factors that have led to an identity crisis for information service centers and the information professions points toward the need for a radical shift in values for information services. The model proposed in Chapter 8 shows the need to identify the different tiers of information services, from generic to enhanced.

There is no easy way for the lay person to learn quickly about information resources, their supporting technologies, and the information service industry. Information scientists, librarians, computing professionals, data processing specialists, and telecommunications experts are the information workers who, with their research and writings, could fill the void. They do not. They write not to explain to outsiders what they do, but primarily to develop a growing body of literature that deepens their own understanding of the field. Up until the 1980s, in fact, the literature of these intersecting disciplines seldom 'crossed the street'.

Most of the journal and monograph literature about information systems and services is scholarly in nature and rife with a professional jargon. At times *Nature*, *Scientific American*, the *Wall Street Journal*, or the *New York Times* will have articles that explain aspects of the information explosion, new information technology, or telecommunications connections around the world.

These scattered items provide pieces of the puzzle. There is no single guide that can take an analytical reader from A to Z with a view to making tough decisions about information services – until now.

There are some related works that may help those who want to explore specific aspects of the subjects in this book more deeply. Among titles listed in the bibliography, Ascher's (1987) book examines outsourcing, or contracting out, but from a British perspective, with emphasis on service industries in both the private and public sectors. There is no specific mention of information or library services, however. Murdick, Bender and Russell's work (1990) has a chapter on technology and information systems. Their work is a text, however, and is limited to a discussion of how information technology and systems contribute to planning and operating service industries. Another British book by Mosco, *The Pay-per Society* (1989), has an intriguing title and is a discourse about the use of electronic media and computers to expand financial and social control and the impact this has on societal values.

Unless an individual is willing to search for journal literature across a wide variety of disciplines (viz. management, computing, and information and library science) then this book is the best source of help. Barring that, an experienced consultant can be helpful to organizations in search of the bottom line for information services.

2 In-house information services

◆ Operating in-house services
◆ Clash of values
◆ Outsourcing
◆ The good and the bad
◆ Financial implications

Information centers or libraries are most often viewed as whole organisms comprised of inter-related units. Managers of those units would certainly argue that their operations are so intertwined that component parts cannot be segregated. They claim that the operations of acquisition, organization, retrieval, and dissemination of information cannot be separated from one another without damaging their capacity to deliver information when needed. Should executive decision-makers accept these arguments? And if so, what should they know about operating in-house information centers/libraries? Is there a 'best way' to ensure minimum cost but a high yield from this investment? Where does this glob of 'soft' services fit within the organization? These kinds of questions can best be answered by first characterizing the nature and values of information services and then exploring two ways to have an on-site information capacity: (a) using an in-house operation; and (b) contracting out the entire information service system.

◆ Operating in-house information services

Only a small number of people outside the information professions knows what goes on in a library and about its service capabilities. The more who know about both, the better an information center is able to survive through years of down-sizing and cost-containment. With rare exceptions, libraries and information centers are not the creators and generators of information or knowledge. They are, instead, the consumers of the information industries. In this

9

context, information professionals in an organizational setting have distinctive roles. They scour the world for information that they feel is important to the client groups they serve. They select the information most meaningful at present or likely to be in the future and either buy or trade to get it. Once they have received it, they categorize it, sometimes analyzing the content of containers so that tid-bits of information can be found at a later date. These functions are rather like an expanded but more formally organized version of the human mind: it collects experiences and knowledge and then retrieves and applies them to new situations, problems, and events when needed.

For information centers and libraries, the universe of information that exists is immense. For example, over 600 000 new book titles are issued every year around the globe. An estimated 45 million records in an array of subjects that cover the world's knowledge are created each year by the 70 firms that are members of the National Federation of Abstracting and Information Services in the United States. From this universe, the information professional must determine what should be bought to maintain a collection of information relevant to the constituency served. Since most have a finite and insufficient amount of money with which to buy information, decisions of relevancy are far from easy. The reliability of the source of the information, the verifiability of the information, the currency of the information, the potential short-term and long-term useful life of the information, and the actual versus dormant need for the information are all factors that must be considered in the seemingly simple process of 'selecting' information. Most often it is librarians which perform these functions. In some environments, the clients have a great deal of say in the selection of information. Without central and professional decisions, however, client-controlled selection can skew the collection toward individual short-term interests at the expense of a focus on the needs of the total organization. Astute information professionals will know how to balance local and short-term interests against broader and future needs.

The actual information order or acquisition process is usually assisted by information technology, viz. online verification of sources of information, and transmission of orders through electronic message systems. Like most other businesses, the information world has wholesalers that specialize in filling orders for books and other information containers such as journals, databases, and video tapes, to name a few. Knowledge of the best (fastest, deepest discount, specialty houses) source of information is another skill that qualified professionals bring to in-house information center operations.

Once obtained, information containers must be housed somewhere in the organization. Since they cannot just be kept in helter-skelter order, they must somehow be indexed and grouped much like office files. Because designation of 'file headings' to the world of information is understandably complex, manual and computer-assisted systems have been devised that provide a framework for organizing the world's intellectual output. Thesaurus control of terms, formats for entering descriptions of information containers, and methods for classifying information are all systems devised by information professionals to expedite these functions. Such systems are usually governed by internationally accepted standards that spare each site from reinventing the wheel and enable some cost-savings to occur. The actual work of classifying and filing/shelving information in an information center is often done by trained para-professionals under the guidance of an information expert such as a librarian. By using descriptions and classification categories assigned by others, a local information professional can speed up local processing and organization of information tremendously. Both profit and non-profit organizations provide access to shared databases that provide copies of previously created records.

Housing a collection of information means that an organization must commit physical space and specialized furnishings and equipment to the operation. To provide access to information in various kinds of containers requires, as shown later, that the site be outfitted with specialized equipment. Standard office furniture will not suffice for an information operation as yet. Until the day arrives that there are virtual electronic libraries 'without walls', the paper on which most information is currently contained will require shelving, floors stressed for heavier-than-average loads, computers and telecommunications lines for organization and access to information and for linkages to the external sources of information, as well as format specific equipment (e.g. microform readers and printers, audio-visual playback units, and computers). In terms of planning, it also means that organizations must commit to future growth in the amount of space used by the information enterprise, particularly if most of the information containers used in the organization continue to be in paper form. While futurists might say that all paper will soon be replaced by electronically stored and transmitted information, the effect of this transformation has yet to be felt. Few collections of information that exist today have a 'no-growth' policy and are able to maintain a static size. In Chapter 8 the notion of the library no longer being centered in a physical space is more fully discussed. For planning purposes in the 1990s, however, space is an overhead cost that must be taken into consideration in operating an in-house information service.

Those who make funding decisions about libraries often characterize them as bottomless pits that can swallow up an infinite amount of money. This is primarily because the world of information available far outstrips the capacity of a single information center to corner even a small amount of information about a highly precise topic. Thus, information professionals must also know where to find information, particularly that which is not available locally. Knowledge such as this means knowing which of thousands of text and bibliographic databases will be the best source(s). It also extends to knowing how to get access to the databases (i.e. which roads to use) and how to structure cost-effective searches of the databases themselves. In terms of road travel, the equivalent would be travelling from one small town to another with each using their own language, their own traffic rules, and their own sign systems. Imagine driving into a town where a blue light at a traffic signal meant 'stop'! Since there is as yet no standard 'language' that is used by various creators and vendors of such databases, considerable skill is needed to navigate successfully through them. Retrieval and dissemination of information then, are the publicly visible partners of the selection and acquisition functions of information service centers.

With the advent of computing and telecommunications, access to some information sources has become available on a direct purchase basis. Telephone information services such as those offered through the 'Donnelly Talking Yellow Pages'[1] in the United

---

[1] The Donnelly Directory is a company of Dun & Bradstreet. Through the telephone system it provides oral information that rivals a public library's quick information or telephone reference service. Access is provided to the Dow Jones Voice Information Network that provides current information about business news headlines, stock market trading summaries, Dow Jones industrial, transportation, utility, and composite averages, and trading reports on the bond market, precious metals, foreign stock markets, major American stock

States are very similar to information services provided by public libraries. Individuals who subscribe to network services such as *Compuserve* or *Prodigy* can have direct access (for a fee, of course) to the same databases that librarians have traditionally viewed as being exclusively in their purview. Encyclopedias and other information sources are now packed onto compact disks (CDs) in digital form. These again encourage individual use without the help of an intermediary. A growing number of people find them relatively easy to use and sufficient for their needs. Others, needing more in-depth information, would rather turn over a set of specifications to a professional and be presented with the results of a thorough search for information. To date, the need for specialized equipment (a CD drive attached to a microcomputer) has slowed down direct sales of these types of information containers to individuals. When they rival Nintendo in both price level and reliance on existing equipment, the need to use CD information containers in the confines of an information center will be obviated.

In short, the use of information workers to get access to information still prevails mostly because of the number of potential sources of information and the difficulties inherent in (a) finding the right source, and (b) knowing the most cost-effective way to get information out of the sources selected. While the economics of accessing information are discussed in Chapter 4, it is sufficient to say here that, as the technologies now stand, it is more cost-effective to provide access to information through a central information center than to provide individuals with direct admittance. The norm remains to filter requests for information so that local resources are milked before external repositories are explored. Finally, the norm of doing most information service center functions in-house also prevails, although some do 'outsource' selective pieces of their operations, as outlined later in this chapter.

The basic operations of information providers are to do the following with information systems and information resources: select, order, balance money available with best guess of what is going to be asked for, store, maintain at least a container-level

---

exchanges, and commodities. Local information includes lottery results, financial rates, weather forecasts, movie and other entertainment reviews, and lists of local special events.

inventory, catalog and index contents of containers, prepare containers for use, deliver information, promote use and, finally, provide a physical space with furnishings and equipment that facilitate access to information.

It is important to note that concepts of information analysis and evaluation are not normally part of these services. While some corporate information centers do provide evaluations and syntheses tailored to client needs, this practice is not universally accepted. It is also important to note that the range, as well as the depth, of services offered can vary wildly. So can the ease with which libraries can be used. Some are easily structured for use in person or via telecommunications devices. Others are not. Some have built a high level of return business. Others serve a minimum number of people out of their total potential populations. The pricing and budgeting strategies of these centers are covered in Chapter 7.

" In a recent study of working scientists done by the Faxon Institute, it was discovered that more than one in five working scientists say that they read 'less than ten per cent' of the material they felt they should in order to be 'current in their field'. A majority of the respondents, from the fields of genetics, chemistry, and computer science, reported that they read less than half of the material they should in order to be current in the field.

Here is a major need and a major opportunity for knowledge managers. Their clients are experiencing substantial information overload. Whoever develops a practical solution to this pervasive sense of being overwhelmed with information will perform a major service. Who is working on this problem? Who better than professionals in the field of knowledge management?

In order to make a significant contribution in the future, librarians must undertake ongoing programs of basic research and program development focused on the evolving needs of their clients. They need to apply new information technologies to those needs. Without such efforts, the librarianship as a profession will become increasingly marginal in a world in which the management of knowledge is rapidly becoming central to virtually all human endeavors. "

Richard Rowe

The following section outlines value systems that affect the kinds and ranges of services provided by information professionals. The factors and values outlined indicate that many information service organizations, and the professionals that run them, are experiencing an identity crisis. The crisis may make itself evident in various ways in different types of information service organizations, and to differing degrees. Corporate information centers, for example, may feel more quickly than a university library, the shifting priorities of their 'parent' organization. As a result, the need to shift or alter traditional values is being felt with varying intensity.

" The identity crises being experienced by most information services organizations are tied to the larger issues being addressed by companies. Corporations' 'identity crises' manifest themselves as issues such as determining their core product and people competencies, defining the infrastructure required to exploit these competencies and improving overall quality. Clearly, information services does not rank as a burning issue amidst such life and death discussions!

Increasingly, companies are realizing that all of their activities, including information services, need to fit into objectives which are focused on strategic intent. Those organizations which are out front in this regard seem to have developed a hierarchy of analyses to arrive at meaningful levels of expenditures for their staff functions.

At level one, companies define their strategic intent and the competencies they need to accomplish that intent. This provides a framework within which to ask questions such as: what information will be required to accomplish our strategic intent? The resultant environment is one in which services are 'pulled' from the business rather than being 'pushed' from information services organizations.

The next level of analysis deals with infrastructure. Once companies have a well-focused intent and objectives, it becomes appropriate to define the infrastructure which must be in place to accomplish goals. This process naturally progresses to questions such as: who will provide the infrastructure? how will it be funded? how will it operate and who will operate it?

Information technology infrastructures are in major transition, due primarily to the thrusts to downsize from mainframes to PCs and local area network environments. Until these plans are in place, efforts aimed at applying automation to information content issues will result in marginal payback. This situation is analogous to the difficulty experienced in trying to make the automobile pervasive without adequate highways.

The pressures for quality improvement and corresponding metrics seem to be accelerating management's awareness of the need to engage proactively in information services activities within their firms. The result of this is a good news/ bad news scenario for information services professionals. The good news is that information services organizations, like other staff functions, will increasingly become integrated with the businesses they serve. The bad news is that the information systems people who cannot adapt to the culture of the business will fall by the wayside. "

Michael Cowley

◆ Clash of values

Although the librarian's profession is still relatively young, some traditional values have been infused into the kind of information shops that they run. These values have yielded some of both the good and the bad of information services. Since many of the underlying assumptions of the information professions may be foreign to decision-makers who focus on the bottom line, they are mentioned here. Among the primary tenets are:

- goodness will sell itself
- information should be free
- all information is equally important
- there are no limits to growth

Librarians have not been schooled to think in cost-benefit terms. For the most part they are in charge of operations that are not separate legal entities and hence may have no real sense of fiduciary obligations. Overhead costs are often buried in the parent organization. The primary focus of the profession has been on the collection of information, not on accountability and the quality of service. Information, including opposing views and opinions, should be openly available to all according to democratic principles. Information, if generated out of public funds such as taxes, has typically been understood to belong to the public.

Until recently, (i.e. the past two decades) tradition has imbued librarians with a sense that their services are inherently good and therefore their arguments for funding were much like asking for support of road maintenance – it just had to take place. In the past two decades of economic shifts and changing attitudes toward public services, accountability has become something that information professionals have had to learn to cope with. For those educated in the past ten years, cost justification and concepts such as unit costs are more familiar territory. For the most part however, managerial accounting and bottom line decisions have been alien, if not antithetical, to those who manage information services.

Most information centers focus on counting the number of items they purchase and the number of times those items are used. This has been deemed to be sufficient justification for renewed financial support. Economic analyses of their operations has been rudimentary and has seen most success in examining inputs (ordering materials) and processing (indexing, classifying, labelling, etc.) functions. Outputs, or the retrieval and dissemination of information, remains the least well analyzed information function. Yes, there have been studies that indicate that N number of relevant items are retrieved under certain circumstances. Yes, there have been studies that determine the average cost of retrieval from various sources using sundry techniques. For the most part, however, efforts to describe the value of the information retrieved remain anecdotal, not quantified. Those efforts that have been undertaken were mostly done by economists and have had little impact on the information professions or on decision-making about allocation of resources.

The products and services provided by information centers tend to operate on a service basis. While service industries exist that charge for 'products' and are driven by profit lines, libraries and information centers that exist within the framework of larger institutions are seldom treated as profit centers. In rare instances, other parts of the institution are charged for use of the information center, either through formula allocation or on a usage basis. This, however, is a rarity to date.

Libraries, and usually the organizations that house them, tend to be modeled after what John Scully (1987) has called second wave enterprises. They are focused on mission, not creativity, are hierarchically organized, not fluid and flexible, and are trying to identify their markets and their clients, not creating them.

Times are changing, albeit slowly, so that accountability pressures are being exerted upon typically free public services such as libraries. Units within corporations, when faced with reduced revenues, will seek to reduce expenditures. Libraries, if they charge for their services, will be competing with outside information vendors and entrepreneurs such as those discussed later in this chapter and the next. Examples by governments of privatization of parts of their operations are another signal that the information business, as it has emerged to date, is about to undergo radical change. Products and services that have been ill-defined or have been fuzzily presented to funding agencies will be subjected to increasingly harsher analysis. The questions that accompany these trends are the same ones that have led companies, governments, and individuals to seek contracts for managing all or part of the information enterprise.

Another tenet, that all information is equally important, has had a two-pronged effect on information services. First, it has led to a codification of a professional ethic that dictates that collections of information should contain all points of view on a given issue. In other words, although 'selection' of information does occur there is a conscious effort to ensure that it is not selected with bias or from a prejudicial point of view. This is fine until the point is reached when the information seeker needs guidance in sifting through the pile to root out what is most important or relevant for the question at hand. Except perhaps for information centers serving a discreet group of clients (such as a company), little effort is made to analyze, evaluate, and digest information for clients. Librarians stand back and say 'here is a pile of information, you sift it'.

By the same token, services tend to be passive, not active. While attempts are made to pre-guess needs for the acquisition of materials, few take this value to the service end of operations. Again, in corporate settings where proving value to the company bottom line is important, information professionals will extend their services to include alerting services of forthcoming or newly published information. In educational settings and in publicly operated information centers such as public libraries, such anticipatory and aggressive services are rare. In short, most information centers sit and wait to be asked rather than proactively identifying needs and hustling to meet them – or better yet, creating a market for their wares.

Two other parts of the culture of the information professional that are well entrenched are (a) building for the future, and (b) retention. What is added to the collection of information today becomes the historical record for tomorrow. Retention and preservation of that record is part of the fabric of most information service centers. Success measures by information professionals traditionally have been collection-based and growth-oriented. The more volumes of books added, the better the information center. The larger the collection, the better the chances are that needs can be met locally. These maxims are currently under attack even within the profession but total death will be slow and agonizing. Overcoming the instinct to nurture infinite growth and other values that are ingrained in the information professions will not be easy. The field has yet to figure out how to meld new containers and methods of distributing information with old collection concepts. New measures of success have yet to be developed that can determine how 'wired' information seekers have met with success. So, although dual information service modes currently exist, old yardsticks continue to be used to gauge the effectiveness of information centers – size and continued growth. Yet, these values clash with notions such as cost containment, new output measures, and the shrinkages that prevail in tough economic times.

Information centers are both non income-generating operations, and enterprises that try to build for future needs. Yet they are faced with double digit inflation and are usually seen as all take and non profit-yielding by decision-makers who worry about the bottom line. In many respects this dichotomous view is correct and may be difficult to reconcile. One way to depict the dichotomy of the culture of the profitable enterprise against the traditional information center is to chart values against each other as in Table 2.1 below.

Little wonder that information services are considered mysterious operations and vulnerable to scrutiny. Little surprise also, given these value systems, that hard-nosed managers view information centers as places where controls can be tightened. One tempting way to rein in loose operations is to farm them out in their

Table 2.1 Contrasting values

For profit enterprise	Information center operations
demand-driven	supply-driven
input price	budget allocation
expense distribution	indirect financial control
cash flow	balance budget
unit cost	lack performance measures for 'services'
cost plus recovery	no-fee services
proprietary protection	freedom of access to information
profit	user satisfaction
cost containment	double-digit inflation
market segmentation	global search for information
client-centered	product-centered

entirety. If costs for refuse collection and computer hardware can be reduced through outsourcing and competitive bidding processes, so might information services.

" *Information and knowledge management services are rapidly coming to the forefront of the world's social-economic systems. It is a time when librarians should be coming into their own. Yet they bring to their tasks an orientation which could be their undoing: they have tended to be 'product-oriented' – oriented toward books and journals – rather than being 'client-oriented' – oriented toward the needs of knowledge workers.*

To the extent that information professionals continue to focus on collecting and storing books and journals as their primary mission, they are in danger of being relegated to the sidelines in the information marketplace. Too often they assume and assert that they know what clients want and need. 'Years of experience', they say, provide them with the expertise needed to do everything from establishing budget priorities to designing 'user-friendly' information retrieval systems. There is no greater threat to the field than the assertion of such an attitude toward clients.

As information professionals today, librarians must not be in the 'book and journal' business. They must become experts in understanding and responding to the needs of clients, demand-driven rather than supply-driven. **"**

Richard Rowe

◆ Outsourcing

The 1980s saw development in both Britain and the United States of privatization policies on the part of government that affected many aspects of these publicly supported operations. Information services were not spared when this policy was implemented. The concept of government contracting for services and goods to the private sector was not new. Governmental requests for proposals to have privately owned companies build roads, buildings and weaponry are far from foreign concepts. The trend in the 1980s, however, took a new turn. The concept of 'privatization' that emerged meant that governments intended to turn over to non-government entire sets of activities or parts of activities that were currently being performed by government agencies. This was aimed at service areas that previously had not been encompassed by 'contracting out' agreements. In the United States, the trigger for agencies to consider contracting out their information centers was provided in 1983 when the US Office of Management and Budget issued a revised version of its guidelines for use of the private sector, *Circular A–76*. Before that date, library services had not been included with functions like janitorial services as an activity that could be farmed out.

Both cost-cutting and generation of income are among the reasons for governments and corporations to either contract out or sell off parts of their operations. In Britain, during the Thatcher years, the government transferred ownership of a substantial number of its assets or operations to the private sector. Like the United States, it did so in a variety of guises including total denationalization, deregulation of industry sectors (as in telephone company monopolies in the US), funding operations from fees for services instead of from taxes and, last but not least, simple contracting out for services to be provided by the private sector.

Another buzzword emerged at the same time but was used mostly in the private sector. 'Outsourcing' implies much the same as privatization. Basically, like government contracting out for deliverables, outsourcing means that competitive bidding is used to reduce the cost of operating services.

❝ As companies sort out which parts of their infrastructure are critical to their strategic intent, the components of the

infrastructure that remain become obvious candidates for outsourcing. It is critical for organizations to develop a set of principles to use as criteria for outsourcing decisions. Characteristically, these principles will address economics, security issues, levels of service, fit with strategic direction, and the quality of work-life of employees.

When an outsourcing partner has been selected, it is imperative to involve all parties who will participate in the outsourced functions at the earliest stages of negotiation. One way to ensure a thorough proposal is to have each party independently develop what they consider to be the best agreement and use that as a measurement of the merits of the final agreement. This is referred to as a BATNA (Best Alternative to a Negotiated Agreement) by Fisher and Ury (1981).

Companies that have outsourced critical functions usually find it necessary to maintain a senior staff of knowledgeable people to ensure that the outsourced function continues to evolve within the company's strategic direction and that a proper balance is maintained with short-term issues. **"**

Michael Cowley

Both privatization and outsourcing hold promise of creating a competitive environment that bring economies, efficiencies, and effectiveness in delivery of information services. Another attractive feature of both privatization and outsourcing is that the contracts permit an unprecedented degree of flexibility to change directions, objectives, and services. Both also can result in service that is unresponsive to the parent organization's objectives, since profitability for the contractor can override delivery of services that are not explicitly stated in a contract.

Although not a new phenomenon, privatization of substantial library and information service operations have become much more prevalent in both the government and private sectors today than ever before. In part, the North American free market philosophy coupled with conservative and cost-conscious government attitudes have given impetus to the trend. To illustrate, the US federal government had turned operation of the following libraries over to private contractors by the mid-1980s: Environmental Protection Agency; Department of Housing and Urban Development; Department of Energy. Such decisions did not sit well with some information providers and there was active lobbying against this movement by librarians.[2]

The corporate world is using outsourcing more and more for its network and computing systems operations. Buying from another business with bottom line interest sometimes emanates an aura of guaranteed cost-effectiveness. An organization may pay more but it might also get better service, since contract renewal would most likely hinge on the quality services that have been provided in the past. In addition, there is the possibility that an out-of-house agency has access to a wider pool of talent and resources and thus can better handle diversity in information needs and can respond more quickly to changes in those needs.

Although resistant to privatization and outsourcing of entire information centers, information providers have actually had experience with these concepts within their operations – some of which are explained in more detail in later chapters. For example, information centers have sent, and still do send, materials out to commercial sources for binding, repair, restoration and preservation. They have designed profiles of their needs to give to book jobbers who then select the number and kinds of current publications to be added to collections. They have contracted for data processing to be done that will enable them to convert their traditional card catalogs into a computerized data base. Thus, although the principle of outsourcing has been accepted incrementally, wholesale application to entire information operations has met resistance from those most affected – the information workers. This, and related forms of obtaining information services, is explored further in Chapter 3.

To sum up, outsourcing or contracting out of whole information center operations is possible and has been done. Decision-makers have to be aware, however, that information service center outsourcing is more difficult to handle than a building's janitorial services.

“ *Outsourcing even core functions may enable an organization to focus its internal resources on the most crucial, high-value functions related to the organization's central mission. Thus*

---

[2] The American Library Association, representing 50 000+ members who work in all types of libraries, has lobbied actively against the inclusion of libraries in Circular A–76. Their primary objections are that the quality of information services would deteriorate if whole operations were outsourced or privatized.

many large commercial and manufacturing firms today are contracting out the management and maintenance of their data processing systems to specialty firms. The work gets done better and cheaper. Outsourcing as a general phenomenon is here to stay since it is driven by long-term economic, market and organizational dynamics. **"**

Richard Rowe

◆ The good and the bad

One of the benefits of outsourcing is that previously nebulous operations become well defined through the process of defining specifications and contracts. Knowledgeable negotiators can define clearly the critical success factors that drive renewal or non-renewal of contracts. Another benefit is that costs for the entire operation are fixed for some time, and can be curtailed more easily and naturally than can internal budgets. At times when organizations have little operating budget flexibility, contracts with external agencies are a means by which to ensure fiscal adjustability in the future.

The sources of benefits can also be the sources of difficulty. As mentioned earlier in this chapter, information services are not easy to describe. Thus, it is virtually impossible for someone outside the information professions to specify precisely what the contract should cover. In soft services like information centers, unless the organization has reliable and expert help in defining contract specifications, critical areas might be overlooked. For example, one notorious example in the US was a contract negotiated by the National Oceanic and Atmospheric Administration for a library operation. The agreement neglected to specify that the contractor should buy and maintain a collection of books (White, 1988). If an organization is thinking about contracting out its in-house information center it will likely have lost confidence in management capabilities of that unit. Therefore, it will be necessary to hire outside consultants to help prepare the contract.

Reliable and knowledgeable consultants will be able to identify all services and levels of service that an organization can reasonably expect to achieve, and can help to assess whether bidding companies have the required human resources to deliver

services successfully. Some of the aspects that contract negotiations have to cover include defining responsibilities, costs, and
performance standards for the components of in-house operations
as outlined earlier in this chapter and listed below:

- selection of resources
- order processing
- vendor selection and negotiations
- materials processing
- maintenance of local files and databases
- adherence to national standards
- level of detail in creation of local files and records
- external information access levels and sources
- retrieval and delivery speeds
- additional fees or charges
- special abstracting or indexing services
- user satisfaction measures
- subject or staff expertise
- service types and levels
- reporting level and frequency
- error tolerance
- ownership, replacement, and maintenance of equipment
- space utilization and costs
- locus of responsibility for overhead

In some instances, the entire information center operation has
been cut loose and employees have established what is essentially
a private enterprise which the company then turns around and
engages as an entity. This kind of contractual arrangement, similar
to the employee-leasing that is discussed in Chapter 3, has several
advantages. It enables the information center to function without
loss of corporate memory. It retains a staffed unit that is
knowledgeable about the organization and its needs. At the same
time, from the corporate point of view, it provides future flexibility
to expand, reduce, or eliminate a segment of its operation
depending on the total corporate bottom line picture. Since
information centers are support services and not a central part of
enterprise, this flexibility to grow, shrink, or change direction can
become a significant benefit, particularly to businesses trying to
reposition themselves in the marketplace.

These benefits also point to the dangers of situations where an in-
house operation is eliminated and the entire information service is

outsourced on a competitive basis. There could be loss of institutional memory if one contractor is replaced with another. There is a risk that institutional affiliation and loyalty may be to the contractor, not the contracting agency. There may be no knowledge of user needs or pride in work if the information staff is twice removed from the primary purpose of the organization. From the point of view of one of the traditional role of libraries – maintaining the historical record – it is not yet clear whether contractors will have a commitment to maintaining the integrity and historically significant portions of the collections that they manage. It is also not yet certain how information professionals will handle dual reporting responsibility – one to the private firm and the other to the company manager responsible for managing the contract.

Although it could be spelt out in a contract, the extent to which private contractors will permit public access to the information they manage can also become an issue. This is of particular concern to government information agencies and their roles in supplying the public at large with information about the government. If, for example, a contractor negotiates the right to sell something that was previously provided free of charge, the agency may find that it has de facto changed social policy about information that is generated with taxes. An often articulated fear in the US is that if government information is turned over to the private sector for distribution, the cost of information (created with tax funds) will become prohibitive. It is further argued that only 'sexy' or saleable information will be made available. The consequences are that this selective availability of information will lead to less open sharing of information, and that this will ultimately affect research, development, sharing of knowledge, and the competitive edge of industry, and its productivity.

Another question for negotiators who are outsourcing the whole information shop is the extent to which contractors can get and keep a competent cadre of information professionals. From the information worker's point of view, if they are working for a contractor who has an annually renewable contract, their jobs can never be guaranteed for more than a year at a time. This kind of insecurity is not one that many people can live with, even though their salaries might be marginally higher than if they were hired as regular employees somewhere else. Thus, if offered a job that is not subject to annual contract renewal, there is a good chance they would leave the less secure location.

Finally, there is concern that only those individuals or agencies that can afford to buy information will get any. In short, there will be less fulsome or even inaccurate information disseminated to those who pay less. To some extent this phenomenon is already being seen in traditional libraries. These typically limit the amount of information that they supply to users from online database searches. Most have a maximum amount of information that they will provide at no cost to users. If they are required to do a full and thorough search, the user is usually asked to pay. In outsourcing situations, contracts might place a limit on the total amount of information queries or searches that will be provided, leaving unimpeded access to information at risk.

◆ Financial implications

Whether an information center is operated as an in-house service or is contracted out, use of funds are comparable. Most information centers have money problems. The largest segments of their budgets are for salaries and benefits. These are virtually fixed costs. The next largest portions of expenses are for the information itself – the books, the journals, the data files, access to remote databases. In this category, rapid technological changes are challenging traditional values and resources. The new technologies are not seen by information professionals as supplanting traditional book and journal collections. They have incurred add-on costs that have been handled without additional funds being made available. Costs for acquisitions are semi-fixed costs. While reports and monographs ordering can be controlled, getting rid of memberships, service contracts for database access and subscriptions to magazines take almost as much time as it does to fire an employee. For this reason, acquisition budgets have seldom had enough elasticity to absorb the need for new information containers and technologies.

Other costs regularly incurred by information centers regularly include outside services such as use fees, annual fees, connect charges and memberships in organizations that enable access to shared pools of information for purposes of borrowing materials not held locally. Participation in consortia can bring some tangible benefits through special rates for volume use, for which smaller centers would not otherwise qualify. Telecommunications costs and computing equipment can either be part of the information center's budget or can be supplied by the parent organization. Other smaller financial commitments needed to operate an information center include, of course, supplies and sundry expenses such as hiring outsiders to do technical and specialist tasks.

If an entire information center is outsourced, the organization will benefit from being able to determine the total cost of the operation. Outsourcing the entire entity will not be much help in determining unit costs for specific information functions, however. It may be easier to control some costs, such as access to value-added networks' information services, but measuring the bottom line by fiscal savings alone will not provide guidance about the effectiveness of in-house versus outsourced information services.

The following table summarizes the degree of fiscal flexibility and amount of overhead commitments attached to several options.

Table 2.2 Fiscal flexibility

Options	Fiscal flexibility	Overhead commitment
in-house full service center	low	high
outsourced operation	high	low
ad hoc distributed resources	low	medium
distributed services	low	high
information brokers	high	low

In-house and outsourcing operation of entire information service centers are diametric opposites – the former allows a high degree of fiscal flexibility and lower overhead commitments; the latter demands high overhead costs and a relatively low degree of fiscal flexibility. Distributing information resources throughout an organization on an ad hoc basis without accompanying service personnel, results in lack of central control of fiscal outlay and therefore relatively low levels of flexibility. The overhead commitments in this option can vary depending on the quantities involved, hence they can result in medium overhead requirements. A distributed, but centrally controlled service center will most likely mean that fiscal flexibility and overhead costs are much the same as the operation of an in-house full service center. The option of using information brokers, more fully explored in Chapter 3, results in a different and possibly more appealing option: a high level of flexibility and low overhead requirements.

So far, two options for information services have been discussed. Both have benefits; both have problems. The following chapters discuss various pieces of the pie: the information workers, the information technologies; the search for information; the internal processing of information tailored to suit an organization's needs. From the point of view of human resources management, there are also a number of options available, ranging from use of resident staff, to dispersion of various components to other units, and to the use of telecommuters and information brokers to buy services as needed.

In reviewing the options in this and other chapters, decision-makers naturally have to consider the short-term impact as well as long-term implications of their decisions. They must also consider the effect of their decisions on remaining inside the organization. The next chapter explores some of the human factors more thoroughly. Above all, decision-makers must pre-guess what changes in information services, systems, and technologies will mean to the strategic direction of the entire organization. It is difficult to argue against information being key to any organization. Thus an understanding of information service centers is mandatory before irreversible decisions are made about these operations.

3 Information workers

◆ Leasing employees
◆ Temporary specialists
◆ Information brokers
◆ Telecommuting
◆ Management options

In recent years, information workers have become caught in a maelstrom of outsourcing and leasing arrangements. Because of this, they have begun to experience working lives as temporaries, leased employees, and telecommuters. This chapter explores the type of staffing and management models that can provide information services as an alternative to the permanent cadre that was discussed in Chapter 2.

Traditionally, information services have been provided largely by full-time career employees such as librarians, information scientists or software engineers, working for organizations as full-time career employees. As was pointed out in Chapter 2, the information centers in which these professionals operate have traditionally been part of a larger organization or in-house units. Like most other skilled white-collar workers, information employees are hired to do a specific job, they adapt to function in a specific environment and, assuming adequate evaluations, can stay forever. Accordingly, they can become stagnant and, with time, retire. Due to both tradition and the complexity of the tasks and technologies involved in information services, typically one-fourth to one-third of these individuals will be professionals such as librarians or information scientists.

As with other professional service employees, a group of information workers such as librarians will have a higher level of education, have more responsibility and autonomy, and be compensated better[1] than the average service employee. Until

---

[1] Information service employees' salaries can range from relatively low salaries to fairly high. Some traditional librarians have an almost missionary dedication that will lead them to work for relatively low salaries. At the other end of the salary spectrum might be computer applications specialists who can command extremely high salaries from a market in which their skills are rare.

recently, information workers have tended not to be used by organizations as contingent employees – viz. employees that are part-time or temporary. There are few independent information professionals that function outside an employee–employer context. Similarly, telecommuting, although having grown at a phenomenal rate in the last ten years, has yet to catch fire in library and information service operations. Visions of knowledge robots that can function as personal information servants remain at the visionary stage. A key question then remains about how best to organize information workers so that information systems, resources and technologies are used to their fullest capacities.

" Knowledge creators and knowledge users need a lot of help in managing information and knowledge. It will be a long time before there are personal automated software 'knowbots' smart enough to anticipate, and find and deliver information as well as a really good reference librarian can. Until that time, it is important for librarians to move out of the 'back room' and concentrate upon client services. Librarians need to concentrate their scarce resources on providing their clients with 'smart' services – analytic studies, surveys of the literature, current awareness services, and customized databases. Contracting out of technical services functions through the use of specialized software systems, off-site and on-site ordering and check-in services, can free up librarians to be more visible to their clients.

Librarians must become more focused on providing their users with the information they need, when they need it, rather than managing a 'collection' of materials that are present if, and when, their users might want them. Users have relatively little appreciation of or interest in what goes on in the 'back room' of a library.

In order for librarians to obtain the financial backing they need for their services, they must increase their perceived value to users. Their 'just in case' values must give way to a 'just in time' orientation that is organized around the ability to deliver information from a variety of sources, only a small percentage of which will be physically 'on site'. "

Richard Rowe

Several models exist for using information workers as contingent employees to staff information service functions. These alternatives include leasing and hiring them on contract. They also can be hired as temporaries like so many office and manual laborers are. A more radical option is to buy information services, as needed, from independent information brokers/workers. Each of these options is discussed in turn.

◆ Leasing employees

Outsourcing an entire operation, as was pointed out in Chapter 2, is an option that can result in cost containment, added value, rapid results without a long developmental period, as well as enhanced flexibility to respond to change. Outsourcing parts of the information resource functions can achieve the same end. In both models, the most important success factors are careful definition of the functions that need to be outsourced, delineation of the extent of control to be exercised and, of course, finding the appropriate provider for the services.

Outsourcing and leasing employees to provide portions of information services are similar since they both allow better control of costs, can effect change more easily, and permit the organization more dedicated focus on its prime mission. Leased employees are usually hired through companies work as follows: a business enters into an agreement with a leasing company that hires all or some of the existing employees and then leases their services back to the business. This leaves the leasing firm responsible for hiring, firing, and managing the personnel. The enterprise is relieved of all employee-related functions such as payroll, health-benefit administration, tax preparation, and other employee-related management administrivia such as paperwork. The costs of leasing can range from 15 to 36 per cent of gross payroll. For most employers this means significant savings on the costs incurred for employee administration.[2] The transition from employee to contractual leasing also often provides an opportunity to shed unproductive employees and operations that are of marginal relevance.

---

[2] The average business in the US spends 39 per cent of gross payroll on employee administration and benefits plus an additional 10 per cent on recruitment and turnover. This and the remaining factual information about employee leasing comes from 'Affording a staff' (1990).

From the engaging partner's point of view, leasing employees is an option that avoids committing a large portion of time to managing operations that are peripheral to their principal purpose. Information service and information operations are natural targets for leasing for this reason. Leased staff can provide a source of instant expertise while someone else does the hiring, checks references, negotiates salaries, and dismisses employees if performance is not satisfactory. This can be particularly useful in smaller settings where line managers are often not knowledgeable enough to hire specialists such as information workers.

From the employee's point of view, working for a leasing firm can have definite advantages. Sometimes employee-leasing companies can provide employees with improved benefit packages and more job security than they had before. Improvements in benefits can in turn lead to lower turnover rates and consequently less time and money spent on recruitment, hiring, and training new employees. A move to an outsourcing vendor can also mean that both vertical and horizontal career movement is opened up. Employees with a specific interest may often cross over to other areas, and can expand their careers both within the leasing company and within client organizations. Many outsourcing vendors also offer enhanced training and educational opportunities in order to keep their most competent employees in what is acknowledged to be a more demanding environment.

The concept of employee leasing has seen rapid growth in North America. By 1990, the number of employee-leasing companies had reached 500 and the number of employees, 300 000. The National Staff Leasing Association was formed in 1984 to regulate the industry. To date, employee leasing has not permeated widely into the public sector or information centers. Libraries and information services, however, particularly in the private sector, do meet several of the criteria that have led businesses to enter into employee leasing agreements: they are operations that are secondary to the prime mission of the organization; and they require the management of a cadre of specialists. For these basic reasons, information centers appear to be ripe for plucking by leasing companies.

Outright employee leasing as well as the use of lease-for-hire can reduce the risks in hiring regular personnel for some organizations. Leasing or outsourcing can also speed up the hiring process. Most lease-for-hire personnel arrangements resemble leasing a car with an option to buy. The City of Los Angeles used this technique to overcome the problems associated with rapid growth in its communications networks, at a time when experienced specialists in data communications diagnostics and trouble-shooting were in short supply.

As Hand (1988) describes their experience, it was a great success. Five options were considered. The obvious one, hiring through regular civil service channels, was rejected as too slow and inappropriate because the City's personnel department was not equipped to handle specialty recruitment efforts. A second option was hiring through a recruiting firm or a head-hunter. While this process would have been faster and might have yielded a better pool of candidates, fees would have to be paid to the agency with little guarantee that the employees hired would be acceptable in the long run. A third, rejected option was to promote or transfer people from other projects or departments. Apparently the difficulties of replacing them, and the potential lack of interest, would not provide enough of a guarantee that the skills sought would in fact materialize. Straight contracting out was rejected because the city really wanted communications specialists with some longevity, not just expertise that would disappear at the end of the contract period.

The final choice, lease-for-hire, enabled the city to work with a data processing service firm that in turn worked with a recruiter to search nationally for the requisite skills and experience. Subject to interviews and reference checks by the data processing firm, two employees were leased to the city with an option to hire within nine months. In that period of time the employer had the opportunity to assess the individuals and, if the project did not work, the City could simply sever the contract with the leasing company.

While not a solution for everyone, lease-for-hire can be a fast way to provide an organization with qualified and potentially long-term personnel. Since leased employees can also be added to the regular payroll at the end of the lease, some of the problems that are inherent in the use of temporary or part-time employees can be avoided. Lease-for-hire, like outright employee leasing, is not a concept that has seen much application in library and information services. As information centers become more technologically intensive, however, and as the pool of skilled workers shrinks, lease-for-hire may see more application in these kinds of settings.

◆ Temporary specialists

As with the other forms of contingent employees described so far, temporary information workers are reluctantly used. This practise is almost anomalous in most information service operations even though it is common practice in the private sector. Granted, information centers have hired temporary employees to fill in at peak times or during vacations. In the past however, these have tended either to be clerical (office help) or manual labor (book shelvers). If the temporary employees were skilled professionals, they were often former employees who 'knew the ropes'. With the advent of computing came the need for people who could operate specific computing hardware or software, who could install or fix specialized information systems, or who could train regular employees to use various kinds of systems and networks. With such skills in short supply and high demand, temporary employment arrangements or short-term contracts became more acceptable.

In addition, in the not-for-profit sector, the past few decades have seen increasing reliance on grant funding to augment operating budgets. This has resulted in information service operations placing increasing reliance on temporary employees, either to replace regular staff who complete the grant-funded project, or to do special tasks for which there is no resident expertise. Typical uses of temporary employees in information service centers have included projects such as data conversion, building and designing access systems, designing and presenting user education, cataloging of special types of materials, searching databases, and doing special studies – all functions that need higher levels of education, skill, and experience than the typical contingent worker.

In an economically uncertain climate, hiring of temporaries has benefits similar to the use of leased staff. It is a way to alleviate staff shortages without incurring a long-term financial commitment. Businesses make regular use of temporary hiring for this reason. The fiscal flexibility and the ability to respond to market demand and supply fluctuations have been self-evident. Information service operations without a bottom line to worry about, have never been affected much by such factors, except in corporate settings. In-year budget cuts and recurring annual budget reductions are, however, forcing information service operations to identify new staffing patterns.

Individuals who work as temporaries see flexibility as one of the perquisites of their jobs. This is of particular value to working parents, retirees, and those who place high value on free time for travel and leisure activities. In addition, from the point of view of retirees and others who want temporary and part-time work, they can usually earn the same salary on an hourly basis as do full-time employees. Sometimes, former permanent or salaried workers earn more on a temporary or hourly basis than they do in regular jobs. This is because they have the leeway to work longer hours and bargain for their rates (provided their performances warrant it). If they work under the umbrella of a temporary placement/ employment company, individuals may be provided with paid vacations and holidays, health benefits, life insurance, and pensions that rival most regular employment situations.

The problem with use of temporaries in highly skilled occupations, such as information services, is that the expertise is lost at the end of the contract period. In addition, there are times when the pool of temporaries needed (e.g. automation experts, indexers and catalogers) simply may not exist.

There are agencies that specialize in providing information workers either as temporaries or on a contractual basis. In the United States, for example, Pro Libra Associates Inc. (6 Inwood Place, Maplewood, New Jersey) and C. Berger and Company (P.O. Box 274, Wheaton, Illinois) specialize in supplying temporary workers to staff libraries and information centers either on a continuing basis or on a project basis. These types of firms advertise that they have special expertise in areas such as selection and evaluation of materials for collections, planning, administration, retrospective conversion of records, cataloging, and training programs.

The private sector's experience with the use of temporary workers has led the way, and can provide libraries and information centers with enough models to make this a viable staffing option for all sizes of operations. Even though some larger libraries have used temporaries for some time (usually under the guise of grant-funded special project staff), shrinking budgets are dictating a philosophical shift toward the hiring of a flexible cadre of highly skilled specialists such as information analysts and database navigators, mostly to be hired as needed on a temporary basis.

With the information technologies changing so rapidly, the use of temporary workers may be the best way to ensure that the most current expertise is available to the organization when it is needed. A retinue of permanent staff may be hard-pressed to sustain expertise in the long-term in a field that is experiencing volatile changes in technology, software, and information delivery mechanisms. A model developed for the future research library (Woodsworth et al., 1989) predicted the need for much more staffing flexibility in response to changing research and educational agendas within the academy. There is no reason to think that other settings will not experience the same need for increased flexibility. In the corporate world, research and product development directions (and concomitant staff expertise) often are altered rapidly in response to market needs. Therefore they too may need to rely more and more on information specialists with different subject backgrounds or different information technology skills as their operations are redirected. This again argues for increased use of temporary employees along with other contingent staffing models.

Thus, fiscal flexibility as well as responsiveness to client needs argue for the development of pools of information specialists who can be hired on a temporary basis. Ultimately, this may mean the evolution of groups of itinerant information workers who function much like the master craftsmen of the Middle Ages – travelling from place to place plying their highly specialized trades. The difference is that many of today's information 'masters' can travel via the electronic highways described in Chapter 6. By now it should be apparent that the advantages of using temporary staff are many. Disadvantages do exist and are discussed later.

◆ Contracting with information brokers

In 1988, Manufacturers Hanover announced that it was closing its 10 000 volume library and laying off its eight information employees. A spokesman said that 'Whatever information is necessary in the future by employees can be obtained through external databases . . .' ('Hanover closes library . . .', 1988). The same article pointed to a similar closure at Bankers Trust in the late 1970s, indicating that employees in future would rely on electronic data bases and ad hoc collections of books and documents. Money & Investing carried a feature in 1989 about the Securities and Exchange Commission's (SEC) closure of its New York and Chicago reference rooms (Winkler, 1989). The repercussions of this closure were that investors, accountants, lawyers, professors, and students who were daily users of the service were forced to use other sources of information. Among those are, no doubt, the information service provided by information brokers.

It was assumed by Hanover, SEC, and Bankers Trust that the primary quest for information by banking professionals and investors is not for the kinds of secondary information provided in texts. For most professionals, the first need is for current awareness and news; their secondary is for particular, specified information.

" Clients sometimes present lists of their subscriptions to information brokers, with the challenge to reduce this expenditure. Information brokers can rise to this challenge. Replacement of hard copy with online versions will not necessarily effect a cost reduction, but can still introduce economies of scale:

1. Information brokers' searches will include those publications to which the professional now subscribes, and augment them by providing access to numerous expensive and/or esoteric important publications, adding non-print material from databases of broadcasts and telecasts.

2. The information broker can introduce efficiency by disseminating current awareness updates electronically, thus streamlining time and resources. For example, at Inside Information Inc., we operated a pilot project to automate a news clipping service in a government agency. In monitoring 16 topics in three newspapers seven days a week, yielding the total number of 48 searches, the estimated cost per search per newspaper was $1.96. We delivered the results directly to their computer via our private E-mail services, and they subsequently disseminated it to recipients via their internal local area network. Although it did not save money, it eliminated the steps of photocopying multiple copies for internal distribution or faxing multiple copies to numerous separate recipients in remote locations. "

Lois Warren

An alternative to using a resident, in-house information specialist to provide one or both of these, is to hire an information broker to provide these services. Individuals can also, in a limited number of instances, do these kinds of searches themselves. As should be apparent from other chapters in this book, this latter option is seldom as effective as having an information professional, typically called an **information broker** in the trade, provide the required information.

Information brokers primarily serve individuals and companies that lack access to adequate direct or in-house information services. Brokers might also have libraries themselves as clients, particularly if the said libraries lack access to specific databases or do not have the specialized skills needed to handle a particular request.

" *Some librarians, concerned with protecting their position, feel threatened by information brokers, fearing competition or encroachment on their bailiwick. Others who want to provide optimal service to their users, seek out brokers and are a joy to work with. They make heavy use of directories of fee-based services to identify specialists who are able to provide research in a particular geographic area or subject field. L.M. Warren Inc. is frequently asked by law librarians to provide information to resolve legal and insurance cases from world-wide specialist (non-legal) databases.* **"**

Lois Warren

Information brokers can operate as independent freelancers or can be hired from relatively large companies staffed by a number of experts. Brokers' services typically include current awareness services that provide clients with reports on a weekly or other regular basis. The clients specify the topic(s) and the frequency with which they want reports. The broker then 'scans' print, electronic databases, and other sources on behalf of clients and sends them either digests or full-text, again depending on clients' specifications. Another service typically provided by brokers is searching for information on a topic defined by the client. Again, the broker scans government, commercial, and other databases for information and gives the client the results. The 'results' could be either a simple listing of sources or a digest of all of the information located, organized to answer a particular research question. For example, a lawyer handling a case on whiplash, might get either a list of journal articles about medical aspects of whiplash or a list of court precedents. The broker would then be directed to get the full text of the items that seem most relevant. A value-added service provided by some brokers is the analysis and evaluation of the actual information received, presented to the client as a pre-digested and analytical report.

" Clients, whether they are librarians, consultants, or end-users, all appreciate receiving search results in an organized presentation. Librarians do not usually require analysis of the results, consultants usually perform their own, and clients who are end-users like to receive information that has been analyzed, digested, and evaluated. Their preference is not to even read the computer printout, but only the conclusions drawn from the retrieved data. "

Lois Warren

The 'list' service and the current information services provided by brokers are also provided by most corporate and other types of libraries. Only the broker, however, is likely to provide a polished and tailor-made report with distilled information. By synthesizing, evaluating and packaging information, brokers in effect are providing the kinds of hallmark and value-added services that most traditional libraries cannot afford to do on their shoestring budgets. The information broker can typically also guarantee confidentiality and proprietary ownership of the information that is packaged for individual clients.

" A company in need of information of a sensitive nature or on matters of utmost security, finds appealing the information brokers'. guarantees of confidentiality. Brokers have been engaged by multinationals that have large, fully staffed libraries. They may, for example, not wish their own library staff to know the subjects under investigations such as a pending merger or acquisition that can affect the share price of a company's stock. Anonymity is assured when a broker acts as an intermediary. "

Lois Warren

A comparison of broker services with typical non-profit library and information services can probably be best characterized as the difference between a quality service orientation versus civil service orientation. Although many brokers use public and other research

40

libraries for source materials, the tools that they provide to ensure easy access are seldom provided by libraries – even if they provide the same services for a fee. How many libraries, for example, have toll-free lines for their clients? How many accept collect long-distance calls? Information brokering is a growth enterprise, and one that uses existing technologies to their fullest potential: telefacsimile transmission for information, toll-free lines for client access, and electronic mail and database access to a multiplicity of vendors. On the whole, information brokers can compete success-fully against free or library-operated broker services because they tend to have better control of quality and are more conscious of the need to provide superlative service.

" Librarians, even those who perform online searches, think of
themselves as guideposts to information. They exhibit
behavior comparable to that of the traditional librarian who
directs the patron to 'go look in the card catalog'. The client
is still expected to do some work using do-it-yourself
bibliographic tools. But the business person in a hurry is
frustrated by a useless reference to an unavailable
publication. Thus clients go to a broker when speed is
essential. Brokers provide fast turnaround. They understand
that the client wants to know where to buy electrical
components for his Mexican manufacturing plant; not that
page 14 of the August 1989 issue of Mexican Trade Journal
has a price chart, but that a copy has to be borrowed on
interlibrary loan. While the librarian thinks he/she has
satisfied the patron by providing the reference, the broker will
provide the name and address of a supplier. Clients are not
interested in the librarian's virtuoso skill in tracking
references, when they want advice on market expansion.
Brokers are paid to free the client from doing his/her own
work, and they understand that clients do not want to be
directed to a source of information.
    Many are afraid to use brokers' services because of previous
bad experiences with online searches provided by libraries.
They consistently complain that the search was 'too long'.
They were presented with 'the whole book' and had to spend
an inordinate amount of time selecting what was relevant.
Librarians, in their eagerness to satisfy the patron, focus on

quantity. Perhaps they do not feel qualified to exercise discretion and be selective. Perhaps they lack the subject knowledge and hesitate to remove material that might be marginally useful. Information brokers are authorized, and indeed are often requested to do just that. Therefore, the end results are much more focused. Material extraneous to the subject is eliminated with the result that the client is relieved of information overload. Brokers will accommodate clients' requirements by working long hours, and by providing search results in a choice of alternate media and delivery modes. **"**

Lois Warren

There are, of course, broker-like services provided on a break-even and even a profit-making basis operating within both public and academic libraries. Some are set up to serve only the business sector or specific disciplines such as science and technology. Some, like the University of Michigan's service, try to cover all disciplines. The kinds of service provided may vary. Some offer traditional interlibrary services and online database searches. Others border on providing what private information brokers give – document delivery, report writing, translations, consultation – and use marketing techniques to reach their potential clients. Whatever their subject scope, almost all claim that quality service is their aim and that information is provided on a priority basis. Libraries providing such services would seem to be competing directly with information brokers. Many have been established recently in response to the need to recover costs for all but core services, or for services to outsiders.

" *Information brokers provide the 'high end' or 'upmarket' service, while library information services provide 'cut-rate' service. The latter compete directly with information brokers, to the detriment of both, in a contest of cost vs. quality. The discounted, or non-profit service provides 'quick and dirty' searches that are less than comprehensive. Such services may claim to be good quality, but they usually lack access to all of the necessary databases. Therefore the client is deprived of getting complete information and the brokers' clientele is drained away. Most conscientious brokers do not offer services at reduced fees to match that of low cost public service even though they could lose business. Some clients* *are willing to pay a premium for quality and thoroughness, but others settle for economy and use information services that are subsidized by universities, governments, and public libraries. Subsidies fly in the face of a free enterprise system, particularly when the lower cost service is operated with government (taxpayers') funds to compete with the private sector.* **"**

Lois Warren

At present it is difficult to tell what is or will be the impact of information brokers on traditional libraries and vice versa. If there is limited demand for such services, will support for libraries decline if brokers take away their business? Will brokers, if successful due to the quality of their services, put an unwanted spotlight on poor service from traditional outlets such as public libraries? Will salaries of regular employees improve if information brokers set higher values on information delivered? Or will brokers be hampered in charging higher fees due to the existence of free or subsidized (albeit slower and less well packaged) services elsewhere? In Chapter 8 we discuss the kinds of cost elements that are involved in providing information services on a full cost-recovery basis. At present, most traditional libraries that provide broker-type services for a fee, are not recovering their full costs in these services. The values discussed in Chapter 2 are part of the reason. Should full cost-recovery be decreed, it will be interesting to see which will prevail – the independent information broker or the traditional library as a broker. To date neither has a clear market niche.

" *Even if full cost-recovery of a library's information services is mandated, they are unlikely to be fully competitive with the commercial brokers' services. Brokerage within the traditional library may garner the business for 'searches', but brokers will prevail for large, long-term studies and projects. Librarians within the confines of libraries and information centers are not prepared to provide this type of 'hand holding' and proactive research. They are geared toward assembly line reference questions and do not always have time to consider clients' applications and ultimate use of the requested data, but often just fill requests at face value. Information brokerage* businesses *market their services to specific targets such as corporate clients. Libraries on the other hand, continue to 'market' new services the same way they promote the old services – to everyone in sight.* **"**

Lois Warren

◆ Telecommuting

High speed telecommunications systems, pervasive personal computer ownership, and information services are currently in place that enable 'telecommuting' or 'telework'. Individuals can work at home or in offices that are physically distant from managers and co-workers. Through networks, researchers, scholars and businesses are able to confer and provide services faster and more reliably. Although still in its infancy and not yet wholly accepted even in enabling organizations (Hesse and Grantham, 1991), telework has tremendous potential for information workers in the future.

There are models within the information sector for organizations that are considering the use of telecommuting. The Information Access Company in Foster City, California, for example, uses indexers and abstracters to create their databases through telecommuting. Professionals in many walks of life telecommute either totally or partially. Telecommuting saves office space, wear and tear on physical facilities, furnishings, and equipment. It reduces energy consumption, travel time for individuals, lessens pollution and traffic congestion and, last but not least, permits individuals to work according to their biological clock and other demands on their time. Los Angeles has also been the place where two quasi-public remote workplaces, called Telecommuting Workcenters, have opened.[3] Employees travelling to these centers have shorter commuting times, but management is able to retain better control over them than had they telecommuted out of their homes. In these

---

[3] Articles about telecommuting appear with some regularity in publications such as in *Computerworld*, giving testimony to its rising importance. For example, Nash (1991) reported that several Southern California employers share the space, saving employees several hours of commuting time every day.

experimental projects, employees have standard office accoutre-ments, including opportunities for social interaction, provided to them. Employers involved in the project are optimistic that some of the barriers to telecommuting (e.g. direct surveillance and mistrust) can be overcome in this new environment.

Studies have shown that people who use telecommunications technologies adapt faster to other technologies and have greater appreciation of the tools that are used in the information economy as a whole. For information disseminators such as information brokers, librarians and information vendors, telecommuting enables delivery of services independent of the confines of a particular space or a physical collection of materials. This alters the perception that an information service worker must operate from a specific site and places more importance, and reward, on what information they can get access to and how effectively they can use technology to deliver their services and products. To date, the use of telecommuting has not taken hold within the library and information community to any significant degree. Information brokers might be considered to be telecommuters if they rely primarily on electronic access to, and delivery of, information. As Hesse and Grantham (1991) point out in their summary, there are a host of social implications for organizations that shift to tele-workers – ranging from productivity to behavior and managerial presence.

" *A new role emerging for information brokers is to act as a facilitator for telecommuting among their clients. Inside Information Inc. enables executives to communicate with their offices through use of a proprietary electronic mail system in client computers. Interestingly, executives from two of the participating firms requested that the program be installed in their home computers.* "

Lois Warren

For permanent leased, and temporary employees who are providing information services within traditional, book-bound libraries, on-site work remains the norm. With brokers providing services such as those of Inside Information, it appears that entrepreneurial information workers are leapfrogging ahead of traditional libraries in responding to client needs. The commercial sector spends capital to make optimal use of the new and emerging technologies. Library-based information services cannot. They must often wait through budget and decision cycles that delay both acquisition and use of the latest technological developments.

◆ Management options

The options available to ensure that information operations adequately support the mission of the organization pose a number of questions from the organizational and management point of view. One of them is who should manage them, and what does the 'them' of information operations encompass? Even in cases where a decision has been made to outsource information services or libraries, it is presupposed that someone is responsible for other related operations. This may mean a broadening of their responsibilities for monitoring work in other operations such as data processing, paper and voice communications systems, computing systems architecture and development, education and training for use of systems and technologies, office systems, printing and duplicating, records-retention policies and management, reproduction and duplication, and security for all information resources. More importantly, the manager who is responsible for outsourcing information services shifts from being a manager of people to being a manager of contracts – ensuring that the contractor delivers as promised, that work is completed in a timely fashion, and that problems are identified and resolved.

One of the questions that inevitably arises, particularly in larger organizations, is whether or not to create a chief information officer (CIO) position, to be responsible for all information systems and related resources and services. Most of the largest Fortune companies in industrial and service sectors established such positions (Brumm, 1988) in the 1980s. Among the larger institutions of higher education, at least half have decided that a CIO is the preferred route for managing their investment in information technologies (Woodsworth, 1991).

The reasons for creating a position to advise the corporate officers about a myriad of information resource and technology matters will vary with the organization. Reasons may include the need to reorganize for other reasons, the desire for strategic leadership in the technological area, consolidation of competing and overlapping units and functions, the need for consolidated policy guidance, and the need for better control over expenditures and for assessments of the costs and benefits of the information technologies.

" *Placing organizational controls over expenditures on broker services can be achieved by establishing a deposit account. The organization, in effect, purchases a block of time from the information broker. The funds can be used for either or both professional fees and disbursements for online connect-time and associated computer charges. The funds could also be designated to purchase a fixed number of reports, such as a large market study, several moderate-sized, less comprehensive reports, a brief overview, and some selective dissemination of information (SDIs) – daily, weekly, monthly or quarterly. Unlike a subscription, the client usually indicates a willingness to replenish the deposit once the funds are depleted. Sometimes, when the contracting organization is itself a library, broker services can be designated as a 'subscription' for budgetary purposes. If the service is SDI, the finished product can, in fact supplant existing subscriptions.* "

Lois Warren

Other reasons for creating a chief information officer include a desire for budgetary flexibility; the want for better cross-fertilization and development of staff working with overlapping information technologies; the need for improved focus on user needs and the quality of service; and an effort to try to position the organization more competitively through use of the information resources. Smaller organizations might find that an existing manager can assume these functions and thus avoid creating another senior level position.

Some organizations have deliberately not created CIOs either because a diffused management approach works just fine for them, or because there is too much resistance among existing managers to creating a new position and to reorganizing. In addition, some CEOs fear that the creation of a CIO position will mean de facto acceptance of an increased reliance (and expenditure) on the information technologies, not a more rational or cost-effective approach.

When CIO positions are created, existing units that handle various aspects of information operations are inevitably re-organized and are often streamlined or merged. Combinations and mergers might affect any of the following: data processing and communications, systems development, operating systems (including administrative systems such as payroll, decision systems, library and information systems), publications, voice communications, paper mail, user education, copying and reprography, records management, and policy and planning.

Whether or not a CIO position is created, someone in the organization must be responsible for making decisions about the most cost-effective way to staff (or outsource) the information functions. The individual(s) must be knowledgeable about the impact of the various decisions and the capabilities inherent in different staffing configurations. Usually, when entire segments of information service operations have been outsourced in the corporate sector, the chief information officers have been the architects of the plans. Ironically, the remaining responsibilities are often insufficient justification for retaining their positions and their work has been scaled down or eliminated.

As Table 3.1 demonstrates, different attributes are brought to the organization by various types of contingent employees compared with regular employees. While all four types can be used at the same time, different sets of problems need to be addressed. There must be recognition by managers that the human, fiscal, and functional factors combine to form the culture of an information service within the organization. Ultimately, the choice of type of information worker must blend with organizational missions, needs and capacities, and fit with the overall organizational values. Thus, senior managers responsible for information service functions must often make decisions about owning or leasing that are beset with hidden and less than obvious implications.

Clearly, outsourcing of information services is possible in a number of ways. One of those options is to lease them from for-profit leasing firms. Doing so may elicit a more market- and quality-oriented service out of an otherwise passive and generically focused group of employees. Use of brokers can do the same, although organizational controls over the outlay of money on broker services would have to be put in place. Traditional information center settings that are trying to provide both the old and the new (i.e. collection-bound services that are free, along with

Table 3.1 Information worker attributes

Attributes	Regular employees	Leased employees	Temporary employees	Information brokers
Budgetary flexibility	Subject to budgeting system	Periodic w/ contract renewal	Sporadic w/ individual contracts	Continuous
Cost type	Discretionary Fixed	Committed Fixed	Committed Fixed	Controllable
Financial obligation	Long term	Short term	Short term	As incurred
Functional flexibility	Periodic w/ changes	Periodic w/ contract	Periodic w/ termination	As needed
Hiring decisions	By employer	By lease firm	By employer	By client
Organizational commitment	Normal range	Divided	Low	High
Performance measures	Continued/ added support	Contract renewal	Rehired	Quality of service
Supervision needed	Normal range by employer	Normal by lease firm	Above normal by employer	Not applicable
Turnover	Normal range	Normal range	Higher than	Not applicable
Union contracts	Normal range	May prohibit or follow	May prohibit or limit	May prohibit Most silent

broker-type services that are fee-based), have to be aware of the potential clash of values and service attitudes between the two. It is unlikely that one information center can accommodate both kinds of services using the same group of information workers. Chapter 8 discusses this issue further.

4 Resources, services and delivery

♦ **A: Information resources**
♦ The changing marketplace
♦ Runaway prices
♦ The new containers
♦ Acquiring the information
♦ Historical costs = future commitments

♦ **B: Services and delivery**
♦ Access: information about information
♦ Delivery systems
♦ On-demand services

Until computers revolutionized work, all sectors of the information industry (creators, producers, and distributors) were essentially linked by paper and the printed word. Other audio and visual media such as recordings, films, television, and radio had been part of the information chain but, from a traditional information center perspective, providing access to information in print format was their core and justification. In the past several decades, the resources of information services have begun to shift away from traditional print formats toward electronically based ones. These shifts have rocked more than the foundations of the traditional libraries that house collections of books or reports. Publishing operations and marketing strategies have changed. A global information industry has emerged that has the potential to exert unprecedented influence over the availability of the information. The trend to privatization of information has combined with a tighter economic climate and powerful information technologies to force a re-examination of how information resources and services are handled. This chapter and the next discuss the changes that have been wrought and how information resources in new formats are affecting decisions about the very future of information service providers, as well as stimulating different approaches to funding and budgeting.

" The information world is in an evolutionary process that will *take it from archival perspective to one of on-demand access. Historically, information resources were physical entities, stored and acquired locally based upon a local perception of value. Needs were assessed based upon a variety of criteria depending upon the mission of the information center. Information resources were acquired, availability indicated on alphabetically-oriented index cards and shelved to await an individual who needed them.* **"**

Morris Goldstein

◆ The changing marketplace

Information services organizations of all types function within an information marketplace, and that marketplace has completely changed in the past decade. The change has been so drastic that a given organization's ability to maintain traditional levels of acquisitions is being seriously threatened. The situation has moved to the point where the interests of some sectors of the commercial publishing world and those of information service providers are no longer parallel or complementary. The problem has reached a critical stage in the world of higher education in particular, so most of the discussions in this chapter will use this sector to illustrate a possible future for other types of environments.

Many North American campuses are currently seeing an influx of print and other materials into traditional libraries that are at just below 1986 levels. This means that libraries in higher education are using higher percentages of their acquisitions budgets to purchase smaller and smaller percentages of the world's publishing output. Responses to these conditions have included cancellation of high-priced journals, reductions in expenditures on books, and an increased reliance on borrowing rather than buying resources. Since borrowing materials is not without cost, there has been a concomitantly steady increase in the use of funds, previously used to purchase resources, for temporary loans in lieu of ownership.

There are varying reasons for the growing volume and variety of information resources and the correspondingly spectacular increases in their cost; these include:

1. Increases in the world's publishing output;
2. Dramatic fluctuations in currency values world-wide;
3. Escalation in the development of new formats; and
4. Inflation rates for information containers that are consistently higher than average consumer price increases.

Another root of the problem for the US academic community lies in shifting control of the business of scholarly communication to an diminishing number of off-shore companies. An example of this is Elsevier Science Publishers, the world's largest producer of scientific journals, which recently acquired Pergamon Press which in turn publishes more than 400 scientific journals. This marked movement of publication control from academic presses and learned societies to a small group of commercial firms is changing the fiscal power base of the information marketplace, is altering the nature and role of research libraries and, ultimately, the nature of scholarly communication itself. One primary change is a shift in emphasis from ownership of resources to trying to provide access instead.

The forces of supply and demand appear to have gained some influence in the paradigm shifts from ownership to access. Scholars are both producers and consumers of information, publishers are primarily sellers of information, and universities both subsidize and purchase information. Changes in the process of scholarly communication, however, are causing the process to become increasingly dysfunctional. What usually occurs is that information generated within the academy is turned over to commercial publishers, who then sell the information back to information centers within the academy. Each piece of this cycle merits examination.

“ *Scholarly journals represent a challenge. The publishers of these works not only provide current awareness, ease of access, and archival media, but they also provide an orderliness to academia itself. As the arbitrators of significant content, they provide a third-party service that is difficult to replicate or eliminate. As long as academia continues to rely upon these valuable services, it is unlikely that the providers will find it advantageous to modify their policies.* ”

Morris Goldstein

Typically, information that is generated by scholars and researchers in colleges and universities is turned over to commercial publishing firms to be issued in journals, monographs, or databases. Many academic presses and scholarly associations that used to publish journals have given them up as being unprofitable. Meanwhile commercial publishers, particularly in the fields of science and technology, often levy page fees to publish an author's work. This is despite the fact that it is the scholars' and researchers' intellectual work, time, and sponsored research that are the foundation of the ideas and knowledge in the articles being published.

Most authors relinquish their intellectual property rights which means that commercial publishers, not the authors, enjoy copyright protection. With a decrease in government support for research, there are a growing number of alliances between the academic and private sectors which could have a chilling effect on the process of scholarly communication. Some scholars are actually going outside of the peer review stream to commercial interests in order to obtain financial support for their work. In this environment, knowledge becomes proprietary – posing yet another threat to the open dissemination of information. A solution to this might be to adopt the patent model as the means to take back control of the products of the academy's research. To wit, income earned from the patented research findings of a faculty, might be used to take back some of the control of scholarly publishing and reduce its dependence on the commercial publishing sector.

Finally, the information service community buys this scholarship back in the form of journals and other types of publications, mostly at prices that are much higher than an individual would get charged. This means that the academic community is a double investor in some commercial publishers, although the monies contributed probably do not bear an appropriate relationship to the value of the products received. Considering the primary and secondary purposes of publishing and the forces that drive the volume of publications (e.g. reaching a large audience, documenting work accomplished, and personal improvement in status and income), it is apparent that new models of information distribution and access are needed. This need becomes paramount when other trends are considered, such as the rapidly rising prices, particularly for journals, and the new formats and new types of information containers that must be purchased by information centers.

" *Although the information-providing community has made great strides through the use of technology to change the traditional concepts, it is against this backdrop of historical significance that many of today's decisions continue to be made. For example, back 'then', a periodical might have been acquired to satisfy three requirements – current awareness, retrospective research and archival preservation. Today, technology as well as increasing demands and skyrocketing availability have mandated a reconsideration of whether all of the functional requirements can (or should) be served by a single acquisition.*

Instead, a market-sensitive approach points to a hierarchy of information needs that have a plethora of attributes. These attributes include, but are not limited to: price, timeliness, a measure of completeness, a low 'hassle-free' quotient, etc. The user is completely indifferent to the physical location of the information (except as it relates to the 'hassle-free' quotient) or the media on which the information is resident. The information-providing professional must understand this hierarchical pyramid of information needs and fashion the information engine accordingly to satisfy demands.

The model dictates that first, we must publicize the availability of huge resources of information. Second we must create a problem-free methodology to identify and select information in context. And thirdly, we must deliver the problem-solution effectively. "

Morris Goldstein

◆ Runaway prices

Everything always costs more, and information resources are no exception. There are some differences however. Journal subscriptions,[1] still the bread-and-butter sustenance for information

---

[1] Journals are also often called 'serials' by information professionals indicating their periodic and regular appearance. The term 'magazine' is not used here

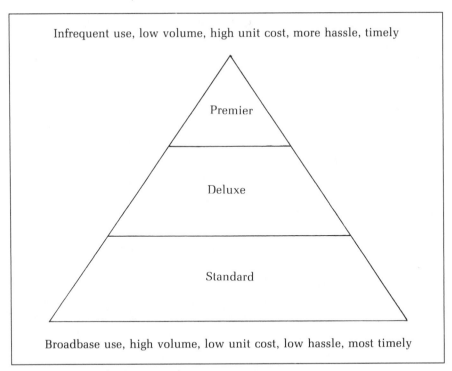

Figure 4.1 Hierarchical pyramid of information need

disseminators and seekers, have been experiencing unprecedented price increases.

An analysis of price increases by Stubbs (1991) indicates that in North America, expenditures for journals by research libraries rose 52 per cent between 1986 and 1990. In the same four years, the number of subscriptions declined and the average prices paid by libraries rose 51 per cent, to a median price of $132.45 for a journal subscription. For some scientific and technical specialties, annual increases have been double digit percentages for the past ten years and average prices are hovering around a thousand US dollars per year.

This phenomenon underscores the bottom line of the information marketplace, as information centers and libraries invest more and more in the commercial publishing sector (a form of partial contracting for information) while buying less from non-

---

since this has more popular connotations than 'journal.' The former might be exemplified by *Elle* and the latter by the *Harvard Business Review*.

commercial publishing houses, including their own campus publishing houses.

While much of the alarm over serials prices is related to scientific and technical information (STI), there are strong indications that other information resources are experiencing similar price increases.

Again, because science and technology is in the forefront of this trend, it is perhaps indicative of the needs in all fields of knowledge. A series of investigations of scientific and technical information needs in the United States[2] concluded that several trends are contributing to the problems of access to STI. These trends are centered around growth in volume of STI, the rising costs of producing the information, the increased commercialization of STI publishing, the emergence of electronic publishing experiments among STI scholars, and the lack of any kind of coordinated information policy on STI. In summary, although the problem manifests itself to information service centers as an uncontrollable financial burden, the solutions are hardly that simple. There is a strong need for national scientific and technical information programs designed to provide ready access to the world's scientific and technical information, be it generated by the academy or industry.

A key ingredient is a shift in the information profession's ethos from ownership to access, as discussed more fully in the next chapter. At the national and international levels a number of solutions are possible. These include:

1. Building the data highways that can provide better access to information about what information exists and where it is located. In the United States this would mean developing the National Research and Education Network (NREN) which is described in Chapter 6.
2. Developing full-text databases in high demand fields such as science and technology – *viz.* providing the means to fill the information silos around the world.
3. Strengthening document depository and document delivery systems or, to continue the highway analogy, ensuring that silos

---

[2] These included studies by the Association of Research Libraries, the National Science Foundation, the Council on Library Resources, the Research Libraries Group, and the Library of Congress.

are available where needed and that roads and maps are in place to fetch fill from the silos upon demand.

4. Finding ways to link resources and information highways between countries without undue taxation and national policy interference or protectionism.

5. Building the public policy foundations that will enable easier and faster distribution of information.[3]

" The concept of a single, comprehensive national electronic library, hinted at but not developed in this chapter, has been around the library community for some time. It is, in many ways, an attractive idea. As with card catalogs, why save more than one copy of anything if you can provide 'instantaneous' access to it through an electronic network? A national, or global, electronic library would appear to solve many of the problems of the cost of information and its management. Everyone could share, in some agreed-upon way, the cost of such a central library.

A critical, probably fatal, weakness of the 'national electronic library' concept is that knowledge is very particular and is most valuable when it is linked with those who know most about the knowledge. What little we are beginning to understand about the way expert systems, human and non-human, work is that they are heavily dependent upon 'the facts' and that these facts are organized and structured in quite unique ways from field to field. Expert systems are made up of a few important intelligence components and lots of knowledge contents. Intelligence is of little value without the content of a field of knowledge. The importance of this 'knowledge principle' is that information needs to be organized around the framework of the disciplines which gave rise to the information and knowledge, rather than kept in some 'neutral' storehouse where it is available to all.

Centers of excellence are needed which provide access to humans who are knowledgeable about the particular field of interest. Library services need to be able to link specialized databases to the people who created them and are continuing

---

[3] In the US, a National Center for Science and Technology Information Services (NCSTIS) has been envisioned as being established within the Library of Congress.

to work on them. Future knowledge systems will be increasingly interactive rather than one-way in nature. This again calls for new knowledge systems that are not just, or even primarily, 'product-oriented' but rather are heavily 'process-oriented', linking people to people.

Future library services will participate in distributed networks of specialized 'knowledge centers', complete with archival information, current databases and real-time linkages to human experts in the field. All libraries will, in that way, be users of other library systems in serving their clients, as well as sources of their own special databases and expertise throughout the global information networks. **"**

Richard Rowe

◆ The new containers

Since Gutenberg invented the printing press, publishers have produced paper-bound information containers that provide the foundation for most information center operations. New containers began to appear approximately a hundred years ago when microfilming was invented. Since then, this format has been used to reduce the space required .by information centers through miniaturizing books, journals, and other paper-based resources. Microfilm and the like still occupied space and needed special equipment to be readable. Similarly, the use of audio and visual media (records, tapes, CDs, films, video tapes) to capture the record of human knowledge brought new types of information containers to libraries and, with them, the need to maintain the machinery to elicit the information. Now, with affordable storage capacity offered by computers, the amount of space needed by information centers is being questioned anew. As with microfilms and audio-visual resources, however, the products of computing technology require the use of more and different equipment in order to make the information resources usable. The technologies are more fully discussed in Chapter 5. This section therefore describes some of the newer information containers and their impact on users, social policy, and the economics of information services.

One of the first dramatic changes in policies and economics of information services was introduced when commercial vendors made on-line databases available for searching on-line in the 1970s. Most of the databases handled by vendors are created by producers who publish traditional print materials from the same databases. While some producers operate their own search engines, the usual pattern is for the producers to lease their databases to vendors such as Dialog in return for royalty payments based on the amount of use.

From the information center end of this process, database searching services brought an unpredictable cost into their operations. Unfettered use of online databases can produce runaway expenditures.[4] For the first time in the history of traditional libraries, they were faced with an information resource for which they could not readily predict their budgetary needs without imposing some sort of controls on access. In addition, the information purchased did not become a permanent addition to the pool of resources available to the broader community – it was turned over to a single user. Budgeting and expensing access to these stores of information therefore created new problems for information service centers.

A minority of organizations built the costs for access to online databases into their operating budgets and absorbed costs on behalf of their users. Free or subsidized database searches (usually limited in scope and frequency) were rationalized on the basis that access to the print equivalents was readily available at no costs to users. Many information centers, including public libraries, adopted the policy that all or part of the costs of online searches would be billed back to individual requestors. After all, the individual would walk away 'owning' the results of the search and the broader community would not benefit from user-specific online searches. The debate about free versus fee based services that was begun in the early 1970s is still raging in the information professions. Basically, institutional policies still govern whether and to what extent costs are recovered for online database searching.

CD-ROMs (Compact Disk-Read Only Memory) made their appearance as information containers in the late 1980s. Initially

---

[4] A year-long experiment with uncontrolled direct user searching of online databases was carried out at the University of Pittsburgh in the mid-1980s. Approximately three months into the experiment, the entire previous year's budget for online database searching had been used. At that point, time limits were imposed and access to some of the more expensive databases such as *Who's Who in America*. (University Library System, 1986)

they contained mostly information about information (e.g. indexes and abstracts) that was already available in both print form and via online commercial databases. CD-ROMs are now appearing as the vehicles for whole texts such as encyclopedias, dictionaries, and other published works. The appearance of CD-ROMs on the market means that the same information is now, more often than not, available in three containers: print and CD-ROM, as well as online databases.

Each of the three present problems for decision-makers. Printed indexes consume a lot of space, are cumbersome to use, and may present only a subset of the entire database. Online searches have potential to be the most complete but are also the most expensive way to access information, and usually require the intervention of an information professional. CD-ROMs need special equipment and can only be used by one person at a time, unless an organization invests in more technology and establishes a network that allows more than one user access at any given time. The biggest difference between CD-ROMS and other information resources are that they are generally not 'owned'.

"Considering CD-ROM as an archival media conflicts with the volatile nature of the technology. The shelf-life of CD-ROMs is not the issue – the constant change in computer hardware and software is. This juggernaut of change is already making obsolete CD-ROM applications that portend to be archival solutions. Thinking of them as 'forever' is a highly risky strategy. The market requires convenient, timely and low cost access to information in products in which quick obsolescence is acceptable. In this environment, CD-ROM excels as a media and will thrive. For storing images forever, it is an ineffective media. "

Morris Goldstein

Printed indices and other print volumes are normally purchased outright by information centers. The results of a database search are owned by the requesting party but ownership of the database itself is vested in its parent company or vendor. With the production of CDs, however, the information industry presented a new approach to information providers – that is to say, they 'own' the disks only as long as they continue to 'subscribe'. Subscriptions are an old concept but with print materials, old issues can be kept in perpetuity even if one stops subscribing. With CD-ROM 'subscriptions', however, came the requirement that all copies of disks have to be returned once a contract is severed. We might consider this to be similar to leasing information, but without an option to buy.

Among the newer and more challenging questions presented by CD-ROMs is whether or not they represent a service or a product, and how an organization can best budget and expense them. Another is whether or not it is economical to cancel the print versions and reduce reliance on online databases that contain the same information. Obviously, information purveyors want none of these things to happen so most have ensured, through pricing strategies, that there are no savings accrued if a print index is canceled in favor of a CD-ROM version. From the point of view of decision-makers who must worry about more than just annual budget projections for information services, the capital requirements for all three types of containers must also be weighed. The cost of housing and storing print volumes must be balanced against investment in terminals needed to access databases, and the disk players, local area networks, and microcomputers needed to use CD-ROM products effectively.

Libraries and other information organizations hold the largest single share of the market for CD-ROM products, and they spend thousands of dollars to 'use' them. CD-ROMs are perceived, therefore, to be a bit more than 'leased' products. They appear to provide value-added services of marginal quality when compared with print sources and to be a more economical alternative to online databases.

Another aspect of CD-ROMs that decision-makers need to watch are the 'service' agreements involved. CD-ROM leases are quite specific about what can and cannot be done with the product. For the most part they do not, however, contain warranties on the performance or quality of their product, e.g. database accuracy, search software, documentation, etc. Like computer software licenses, CD-ROM service or leasing agreements are legal documents addressing such issues as: waivers of immunity; fiscal rules of contracting agencies, including all provisions; amendments; infringements of patents, copyrights or trade secrets; third party access; software ownership; prices and payments; confidentiality; single-user license; updates and replacements; disk return; disk replacement; refund policy; user support; assignment by licensee;

downloading and copying; disassembly; equipment used; term of contract; termination; indemnification; enforcement of agreement; illegality and enforceability; and governing law of the agreement. This is no mean list of potential problem areas. Given the potential legal liabilities associated with the lease of CD-ROMs, many information centers are required to have them reviewed (and sometimes amended) by legal counsel and executed only by authorized individuals.

The regressive aspects of CD-ROMs are that they are intended for one disk-per-user application and are being priced at what appear to be discriminatory prices, much like some journal subscriptions. Local area networks or 'jukebox' access through file servers are solving the first problem. It also seems that some flexibility being introduced by producers in their pricing structures is associated with networking capabilities. Clearly, both information producers and information service centers are groping for solutions that make CD-ROMs a viable information resource.

Another major concern about CD-ROMs is their threat to the traditional role of information centers as collectors and keepers of the historical record. If old disks must be returned when new ones are issued or when a lease is canceled, this clashes directly with traditional archival functions. Worse, it threatens access to older iterations of information. However, since at least one CD-ROM producer (BIOSIS) has changed its lease policy to allow subscribers to retain the year's final disk at no additional charge (whether or not subscriptions are renewed), there is hope that information producers will rethink their policies in this area. Perhaps the kinds of collaboration addressed in Chapter 8 will pave the way for more interactive development of CD-ROM and related information resources.

Electronic publications, particularly journals, represent another new format for dissemination of information. They are another information resource that will probably not be owned by information centers. By way of definition, or description, electronic journals are a collection of articles distributed electronically through data networks. At present there are relatively few, and these exist in text-only format (i.e. do not include graphics or images). Subscribers are free to download all or parts of journal issues. The journals and their articles are archived instantly by their producers and can be accessed by author, title and keyword. To provide quality control, most of these journals' producers use a submission and acceptance process for articles. At present most that exist in the US are produced by the non-profit sector.[5]

Although electronic journals are relatively inexpensive, convenience and accessibility vary with an organization's IS and IT capacity. Institutions must provide the gateways and network access to the computer systems in which they reside, or mount and update the files on local systems. If electronic publications are to be made accessible locally in the same sense as other resources that are owned, then there are real local costs associated with them apart from purchase and subscription charges. In addition to the obvious computing storage and processing costs, integration of electronic journals into collections and services will need continuing investment in computer hardware (and sometimes software), staff training, user education, and publicity.

To date, this format of publication represents only a small portion of information resources and journal subscriptions. This is likely to continue for some time.

For the commercial publishing sector, electronic publications also introduce a series of economical, philosophical and practical questions. Print publishers must accommodate both print and electronic products while containing costs. The process of starting an electronic journal requires development of different marketing and distribution networks. These in turn create additional costs to publishers, which have to be passed on to subscribers. Many publishers depend on advertising to offset some of the cost of publication, and since they are unable to use the same kind of advertising in electronic journals, the costs of publishing goes up. In addition to these factors, the entire process of providing access to their electronic journals requires additional investments by publishers such as:

- ensuring that information about journal contents is available for use on local systems;
- providing pre-publication information on journal contents to indexing and abstracting services;
- producing electronically searchable abstracts; and

---

[5] The characterization of electronic journals is derived from a symposium sponsored by the Association of Research Libraries in the fall of 1990 with editors of electronic journals and representatives from research libraries, systems, university administration, and the university press community as reported by the Association of Research Libraries (1990, p. 7).

- improving the search software associated with their products.

So, while electronic journals may reduce storage costs for some information service centers, these cost reductions may not produce the immediate savings for either them as buyers or the publishers themselves. Even with better access, improved content, compact format, and timeliness of information weighed as benefits against the initial additional costs of electronic publications, libraries and information services are caught in the same price squeeze as that for print journals. Further, it seems that there will not be a large enough number of electronic publications available in the near term (and consequently sufficient competition) to look for lower prices for these publications. Under these circumstances, one cannot look to commercial publishers for electronic publications as the solution to the growing gap between the need for information and the ability to provide it.

For these reasons, it may fall to the non-profit publishing sector to develop an aggressive agenda that uses existing telecommunication networks to create an infrastructure for network-based publishing. This, in the minds of some visionaries, could provide a new paradigm for archiving, quality assurance, preservation, and access to print on demand, at least for scholarly information. Unfortunately, there are currently only 20 to 30 electronic publications produced by various non-profit agencies. They function primarily as pilot projects designed to test various elements of this electronic-publishing access model. For this reason, the quandary of providing access to a growing body of literature in print journals, with a shrivelling pot of money, continues unabated. Doubly troublesome is that the newer formats – the CD-ROM products and electronic whole text publications and databases – are adding another layer of information formats to carry. They are not supplanting traditional ones such as print. While other options for access to information are explored elsewhere in this book, historic patterns of acquiring and organizing information continue to prevail in even the most technologically advanced information centers. So – a new model must be developed.

“ *The new model appears to be more 'market' driven. That is, the ultimate user is indifferent to the residential aspects of the information. First concern is to be aware of the existence of information resources as being helpful to problem solving.*

In other than recreational environments, the user is becoming increasingly aware of the availability of information as solutions. Whether this knowledge is primitive or sophisticated, problem solvers generally know that they need efficient access with minimal interference, including interaction with other humans, precise, yet simple-to-operate tools to help formulate their requirements, accurate descriptions of the available content, and 'rapid' access to solutions to problems. **"**

Morris Goldstein

◆ Acquiring the information

The processes used by most information centers to acquire information containers was described in Chapter 2. Although not normally consciously thought of in this way, one of the most cost-effective ways to get collections of materials has been through outsourcing – i.e. the time-tested practice of using vendors for acquisitions. Public libraries have used vendors to supply temporary use of best sellers. Special and corporate information centers have used vendors to cull the world market for publications on highly specialized topics. Academic settings have used book and journal vendors to handle acquisition of materials according to a set profile – e.g. all output by certain publishers, or all output from certain countries on specific topics.

After a profile has been created of the types of materials an organization wants to receive (and from which publishers), contracts are drawn up with vendors to enter and renew orders for books and serial publications, to prepare and screen invoices, to claim material not received, and to provide additional incidental services such as management information reports. Use of vendors has been especially important for handling journal subscriptions since they enable the management of large numbers of subscriptions without a large staff to process orders, renewals, claims, invoices and correspondence with a very large number of publishers. Journal vendors survive through volume discounts from publishers and service charges to clients (generally a percentage of the total volume of an annual order). For many information centers, this form of outsourcing accounts for at least one half of their acquisitions funds.

Payment arrangements with vendors vary: some have the advantage of early payment incentives, while others require payment on receipt of an annual invoice. Prepayment incentives typically provide credits to the buyer which can be used to offset the cost of subscriptions, add new titles, pay supplemental invoices, etc. Payment strategies can change from year to year, although alterations can affect the vendor's business relationship with publishers.

To permit purchase decisions to pass quickly to vendors, many have developed electronic management and communications systems for their clients. Electronic information exchange expedites renewal authorization on hundreds or thousands of journals, ordering, invoices, account reconciliation, claims for missing or late items, and even orders for printed catalog cards or tapes ready for integration into local systems, at least by large vendors. An example of this is Faxon's announcement in 1991 of Electronic Data Interchange (EDI) as a means for clients, Faxon, and publishers to exchange information about journal orders, invoices, claims, acknowledgements, etc. (Faxon, 1991). The promise of EDI is that it will eliminate 'information float', the time during which the status of shipments, orders, etc. is unknown, while providing real-time publication and shipping notification. EDI should provide cost savings for information centers by reducing the time spent on clerical tasks associated with local inventory control. For example, when EDI is fully implemented, it should eliminate the entire claims process and advance the state-of-the-art to the point where payment for order fulfilment is accomplished through Electronic Fund Transfer (EFT). All such capabilities through the use of information technology should provide economy-of-scale opportunities for clients, vendors and publishers. The obvious questions in the near term are: is EDI an unqualified benefit to all parties? Does vendor-supported EDI serve clients and publishers equally well? Does the current model of publisher discounts to vendors, combined with vendor-generated service charges to clients in an EDI environment justify (and fairly allocate) the continuing cost of contracting with vendors?

One of the most labor-intensive operations in any information service organization is the process of preparing the information resources for local use. Again, as described in Chapter 2, this consists of identifying and describing the intellectual content of each container, and labelling it so that it can be housed somewhere on the premises or, in the case of electronic databases, located through the local/external computing system(s).

Since the late 1970s, many information centers have been contracting with cooperative or commercial firms (e.g. the Online Computer Library Center (OCLC), the Research Libraries Information Network (RLIN), Utlas, Inc. or Baker and Taylor) to provide the 'catalog' records that describe the information containers that they own. These firms currently supply such records in paper form (3 in × 5 in cards) on floppy disks, on CD-ROM, or on computer tapes – all with a view to integrating them into the information center's own card catalog or database.

Libraries around the world have collaborated to build the infrastructure for international cooperative data sharing and have invested a significant amount of time and money in building membership-based bibliographic networks and databases. The result is that there is now access-at-cost to over 38 million of these shared records. While other reasons for collaboration are provided in Chapter 6, the impetus for cooperating to create a shared database for bibliographic records merits explanation. It was basically undertaken to reduce the costs associated with the intellectual work of cataloging. This is accomplished by pooling the records created by member organizations. The results are a freeing-up of local resources (personnel, etc.) to do other tasks or to catalog those materials unique to a given institution.

Collaborative processes such as these are enhanced by both quality control and creation of standards that are maintained by national libraries around the world and the Library of Congress (LC) in the United States. Critical to electronic processing and sharing of bibliographic records is the development of a universal standard for them – known as the MARC (MAchine Readable Cataloging) record format.

Collaboration has added considerable value to the shared databases that are available for use at cost, and can control and reduce costs at the local level. For example, about 25 per cent of the records in the OCLC database are Library of Congress records, and 75 per cent of the records in the database are contributed by member organizations. Creating and copying records to describe new receipts is not the only outsourcing that information centers can undertake in processing their materials, however.

Information service centers can also contract for other services through the cooperative information utilities. For example, if a backlog of materials exists for which there are no data records, an organization can contract with vendors to have electronic records created for those materials. Again, OCLC's services exemplify the options available depending on the degree of staff involvement and financial outlay desired. These services include:

1. **Retrocon** – an organization sends its card file of items owned to OCLC staff and they convert the records to machine readable form, for a fee, usually on a per record basis.
2. **Microcon** – an organization purchases Microcon software and enters its own records onto diskettes that are sent to OCLC for matching against the OCLC database. Matching records are sent on magnetic tape, along with problem reports, again for a fee.
3. **Online retrospective conversion** – an organization performs the conversion itself, using the OCLC database online but at reduced rates.

As with any collaborative enterprise, those involved in maintaining cooperative databases such as RLIN and OCLC, are constantly seeking ways to reduce costs. For example, the Association of Research Libraries in the United States recently began to examine issues related to collaborative cataloging to see if they can increase the number of items for which libraries provide adequate cataloging while reducing duplicate efforts. One possible venue to accomplish this is through use of contract cataloging, whereby some libraries would pay an outside agency to catalog certain categories of materials, such as some foreign languages.

Whether through collaboration or through contracts, outsourcing of both current processing and retrospective data can be a cost-effective means to reduce backlogs, keep processing current and eliminate the need for additional staff.

Smaller information centers are able to process nearly 100 per cent of their collections through the kinds of programs described above. Cooperative utilities and their commercial counterparts therefore provide one of the best examples of providing an effective economy of scale that permits reductions in unit costs.

The pricing schemes for the utilities are generally based on a membership fee, coupled with some form of charge per 'hit' rate, e.g. records used, searches executed, etc., as opposed to connect-time pricing. Connect-time pricing does not necessarily relate to the resources used or the information retrieved, and also discourages heavy use of the interactive nature of the systems provided by the utilities, thereby degrading search quality. Most organizations budget for use of the utilities on the basis of past use and projected extenuating circumstances. Hence the membership fee and 'hit' charge pricing policies of the utilities provide a useful mechanism through which to apply the past-use budgeting process. Expenses for processing materials might, by some decision-makers, be considered to be controllable costs. Most information centers, however, would deem them to be discretionary fixed costs, at best.

Howsoever viewed, the costs of processing and maintaining collections of materials for use are not insubstantial. The historical investment over time and the future costs of sustaining its utility are concepts that executives must juggle in order to determine how much of their information service operations to outsource. For this reason, a discussion about the special problems presented by the older and more traditional information formats is included.

◆ Historical costs = future commitments

Unlike manufacturing inventory, materials acquired to support information services do not get taxed at the end of every fiscal year nor do they necessarily lose their value when newer materials appear. The content of some materials is timeless. The containers as artifacts (such as rare books) often appreciate in value and must be protected against hazards such as ageing, pollution, and abuse by people. Since by far the largest investments (apart from computing and telecommunications systems) by most information centers is in their collection of materials, outsourcing is explored here as an option to protect this historical cost. Repair, binding, and preservation are the most important tasks to achieve this end.

While most organizations perform in-house mending for damaged materials, they do not operate their own bindery. This is an activity that typically is outsourced on a multiple-year contract basis. The multi-year contract is useful as a means to avoid frequent and expensive changes in binding procedures and operations. In addition, if competitive bidding is required, then multi-year contracts can reduce the time involved in outsourcing.

Some of the contract requirements for binding are consistency in quality, quality control, performance-based agreements, and getting the most for the money (economy-of-sale). It is also common-place to require that the binder warrants adherence to accepted standards to ensure adherence to technical and material specifications.[6]

As with other outsourcing activities, a warranty, reference checks, and other standard procedures are critical elements in bids and subsequent contract negotiations. Specific to binding contracts are specifications addressing the type of materials to be bound, the quantity of materials (or amount of funds) involved, the types of covers, labelling, special requirements such as packing and binding patterns/color matching requirements. In addition to the warranty, the contract should also require a statement of insurance against theft, loss or damage, frequency of pick-up and delivery, and the organization's invoicing and packing slip requirements.

Because of the special requirements in both binding and preservation of collections of materials, information centers should be allowed leeway in not being tied to a low-bid rule. Price must be tempered by knowledge of both the quality of the products and the ability to meet special requirements. The same principles apply to outsourcing of microfilming for preservation purposes.

Due to over-use and poor quality paper, many printed works, especially in larger libraries, have outlived their lives even though the information in them is still needed. For this reason, information centers often try to preserve the content of these volumes by having them microfilmed. Although companies are used to reducing their records to micro-formats and storing them for posterity or protection against future audits, the microfilming done by information centers is somewhat different. It is geared to conserving the utility of the intellectual content of an item. Therefore, it is important that these microfilms be of the highest quality possible.

For this reason, many organizations do not outsource their preservation microfilming on a large scale. Not only is it expensive to do (approximately $50.00 per volume) but again, collaborative efforts are under way to ensure that there is as little duplication as possible and that those materials most at risk are in fact preserved. For the most part, it is the largest libraries that are most concerned

---

[6] See, for example, *Library Binding Institute Standard for Library Binding*, 8th edn, (1986), and the *Guide to the Library Binding Institute Standard for Library Binding* (1990), published by the American Library Association.

about retention of the human record as represented in books and journals. They see this as part of their mission. Smaller ones, including information centers in schools and corporate settings, tend not to be concerned about this problem while public libraries span both worlds. At present preservation efforts tend to be *ad hoc* ones with minor pockets of collaboration among some groups of libraries.

Some information professionals also find that the current distributed system (an uncoordinated assortment of private enterprise and collaborative ventures) for filming and access is unfriendly and insufficient. They feel it should be replaced by a centralized distribution service managed by a third party. This is believed to provide more effective and convenient service while facilitating an equitable distribution of costs throughout the information community. If such a plan materialized in future, it would still mean an outsourcing environment for information service organizations that want to house re-formatted materials.

As the new formats (databases, CD-ROMs, laser disks, electronic whole texts) become older, their preservation and access will become major concerns. There are already computer tapes that can no longer be read because no one has preserved the equipment or the programs that were needed to read them. CD-ROMs are reputed to have a shelf-life of seven years. Like the VHS and Betamax videotape battle, a lack of standards for CD-ROM and other information technologies means that inter-operability and future operability are non-existent or, at best, flimsy.

In the meantime, those who want to begin to preserve what they have, Byrne (1986) provides sound guidance for contracting out for microfilming services.

Clearly, a plethora of problems face information centers as they deal with new and old formats for their stores of information resources. Outsourcing has become a way of life even though it is not always recognized as such by the information professions. Yet, the information industry is forcing a re-examination of ownership and access questions by shifting to an information leasing model. This means that information providers will be forced to re-think their customary views of collaboration in areas such as processing and organization of materials, along with how stringently they apply managerial accounting practices to analyze overhead costs for storage, and cost-effectiveness measures for information stores that they tap into as needed or demanded.

As Ascher (1987) points out, one of the reasons for increased reliance on outsourcing is to have increased flexibility in being able to respond to changes in market conditions. Whether as consumers of information or as distributors, the information professions are experiencing unprecedented changes in market conditions. How they are guided to respond by decision-makers in terms of collections has been only briefly explored here. The next section focuses on the service or dissemination end of the business.

    " *A hassle-free environment that enables a problem-solver to feel comfortable with their own information prowess in a very short time is essential to the pyramid of needs shown in Figure 4.1. This stimulates utilization from both the traditional users who expand their needs and the novices that heretofore were intimidated. Only by ensuring easy and open access can we hope to ensure the volume of usage needed to become a viable problem-solver.*

    With the increase in demand, new technology is being employed to distribute content quickly, efficiently and at reasonable cost. This quest for immediate gratification is the final obstacle that is being solved by fax, computer terminals and other high technology. **"**

Morris Goldstein

◆ B: SERVICES AND DELIVERY

Most information seekers who have used traditional libraries are familiar with drawers of cards that indicate what books are located there. Each volume is normally represented by a card for every author, the title, and two or three 'subjects' that depict the content of the work. For many, these catalogs are still the sole doorways to information contained in books. They are usually augmented in almost every library by volumes of indexes and abstracts that hold the key to articles in newspapers, magazines, and scholarly journals. This was B.C. – before computing. Now, a growing number of information centers rely on computing systems and telecommunications networks to give users access to information housed within their own organizations and beyond. The following sections describe the access systems now in place and then outline the delivery mechanisms that augment place-bound collections of materials.

◆ Access: information about information

When information professionals talk about access to information they are more often than not talking about access to information about information. In short they are referring to the catalogs and indexes that point to text, articles, research reports, documents, etc., from which people can get information. Chapters 2 and 4 have described the back-ends of these processes in terms of function and economics. Suffice it to say here, then, that from an information seeker's point of view, it is seldom that any single information center can supply everything that is needed. The typical user of the largest research libraries in North America will have only a fifty to sixty per cent chance of finding a specific item, *if they know what they want*. Most people who use information service centers go in search of information on a topic, not a specific item. Thus their chances of finding something on their topic could be higher – or lower if the topic is esoteric to their immediate environment. To obviate this shallow success rate, information professionals have built an access infrastructure that enables them to find materials that are not locally owned.

One recent innovation that improves access to local collections was the introduction of computing into libraries – to present 'catalog' information on display terminals, to order materials, to control inventory fluctuations due to lending. While many libraries have yet to take this step, some have gone beyond just automating these internal operations and have provided similar online access to databases that contain information about other libraries' collections, indexes to newspapers, and abstracts or digests of the contents of journals and reports. This broadening of online information systems has enabled users to find stores of information resources beyond those that are housed locally.

❝ To provide greater access, a plethora of value-added information products now dot the world. While they tend to be more costly, they have the capacity to expand the scope of any institution's information resources. These are not high technology solutions that merely replicate their predecessors.

73

CD-ROM indexes, for example, enable problem solvers to identify solutions in ways and from resources far beyond the scope of their print and microform predecessors. This is evidenced by a significant rise in document requests from those using these effective tools. **"**

Morris Goldstein

On some academic and corporate campuses, this access has been enhanced by data networks so that users no longer have to come to a place called a library or information center to get access to information. Local area networks, company- or campus-wide information systems, and even interconnected data networks now enable access to information in ever widening domains. The kinds of collaborative connections described earlier in this chapter and in Chapter 6 now provide a backbone (albeit confusing to use) of access to information about information as well as information *per se* that has been unrivalled to date. Users who are intent on finding all there is, can easily be overwhelmed by the array of sources and choices. At a local level they may be faced with a local online catalog terminal, several CD-ROM workstations each with a different information resource mounted on them – an encyclopedia, an index to educational journals, or abstracts of dissertations. Or, if access is from home via modem, the same array of sources and databases might be available through a network. If users are street-smart to the Internet (see Chapter 6), then they have world-wide access to research and academic computing systems and whatever files the participating institutions decide to make openly available.

In this situation it is easy to copy and print as many 'hits' as possible. Where difficulties arise, is getting more than just information about information – i.e. getting the actual information itself either in paper or electronic form.

At home, using local collections and photocopying in lieu of borrowing is one of the most viable means for users to get materials. Photocopying for research purposes, for teaching and learning, and for borrowing and lending among libraries are, for all intents and purposes, a tradition – albeit a tradition still protected by copyright laws in most countries.

To facilitate use and access to materials, many libraries and information centers operate their own copy centers and provide photocopies at cost, often below market prices. Some, recognizing the myriad uses of their materials in facsimile form, have contracted with copying companies to provide these services on-site. The services of these contractors in turn include support for internal uses while operating at a profit.

A recent US court case, however, found a national chain of photocopying stores in violation of publishers' copyright in reproducing excerpts from books and selling them as anthologies to college students ('Photocopying chain . . .', 1991). This points to another challenge for organizations that use contracted copy service. They must find ways to identify and preserve the surviving scope of fair use in their contracts or, better yet, to avoid the profit-margin environment altogether and establish their own at-cost services. One such model is the Center of Scholarly Technology at the University of Southern California. There, a joint library and computing services group at the Center is engaged in an experiment with McGraw-Hill Inc. to produce customized textbooks using electronic publishing technology on a cost-recovery basis ('USC revamps . . .', 1990).

◆ Delivery systems

Apart from the kinds of access changes described above (largely driven by advances in technology), economics is really the driving force that will mandate changes in the way information service organizations operate. As mentioned earlier, the single highest expense for such organizations next to personnel costs is the cost of materials. On a purely economical basis, these organizations will not be able to support the cost of publications in their present or future configurations. It would appear that some form of network-based, distributed information infrastructure will have to be developed, with corresponding new pricing models in publishing.

One such pricing model was developed by Peter Lyman (1990) who envisions a shift to a distributed economic model for publishing, one that would centralize fixed costs and revenues but distribute variable costs and revenues. His model would return the business of actual publishing (authorship, editing, composition, etc.) to publishers while the manufacturing end (printing, binding, distribution, etc.) would be decentralized. The problem with this model is that it fails to consider the variety of traditional and other formats that information service organizations will have to accommodate for some time to come. The distributed network aspect of his model holds promise, however, since information service organizations are already relying on commercial and other document suppliers to supplement, and in some cases supplant, ownership of non-core materials. Allen and Williams (1990) identified several commercial document suppliers which complement an organization's usual sources:

1. ADONIS (Article Delivery Over Network Delivery Service)
2. ARTEMIS (Automated Retrieval of Text from Europe's Multinational Information Service)
3. Scientific Delivery System
4. EIDOS (Electronic Information Delivery Online System)
5. APOLLO (Article Procurement with On Line Local Ordering)
6. Transdoc
7. Knowledge Warehouse
8. Project Mercury
9. ISI's Genuine Article Service
10. The ERIC Document Reproduction Service
11. Chemical Abstracts Service
12. University Microfilms International Document Service

Each of these services provide rapid delivery of facsimiles at a unit cost per facsimile, often as an alternative to the vagaries of traditional interlibrary loan.

The British Library Document Supply Center announced in 1991 that they would provide a Copyright Cleared Service as part of their plan to serve as a centralized source for serials worldwide. In order to make the most cost-effective use of such services, many information centers are experimenting with digital scanning and digital sending, using fiber technology and existing telecommunications networks. For example, the Research Libraries Group (RLG) is testing a document transmission workstation to speed both the document request and the document itself on their way between stations, document suppliers, and scholars (Ariel, 1991).

Perhaps a precursor of the future is the comprehensive current awareness and document delivery system announced in 1991, as a collaborative effort, by Faxon Research Services, Inc. and OCLC. The tables of contents of approximately 10 000 technical, scientific, medical and business journals will be made available through OCLC's network services. A companion service will offer priority document delivery service that will deliver a requested document electronically by 8.00 a.m. if ordered by 9.00 p.m. the previous night. Optional means of document delivery will also be made available.

Each of the applications discussed here will involve some form of charge-back to the requesting organization. Some libraries cover interlibrary loan and/or document supplier costs through their acquisitions budgets, on the premise that they will provide access if they do not own the item. Others are in the experimental stages of studying the economic effects of selected dependence on document delivery as one means of cost containment (Ardis and Croneis, 1987).

" As part of the need to address expanding needs of information consumers, new pricing algorithms will have to prevail. They include fixed-price and unlimited usage scenarios and output driven billing schemes. Each service will be sequenced and prioritized based upon its demand as aggregated via the pyramid of information need shown on page 55. The pyramid operates in a reciprocating manner with high demand content at low unit prices – and vice versa. By understanding this pyramid, information providers will be able to establish more effective pricing scenarios. "

Morris Goldstein

◆ On-demand services

Publishers are beginning to offer innovative means of delivering text in the formats and quantities needed, particularly to educational institutions. This is creating an interesting set of competitive opportunities for bookstores as they see an expanding mission related to the creation, production and distribution of customized products. Advances in electronic publishing technology have made it possible for teachers to order chapters from a publisher's database, add personal handouts to the database and receive a laser-printed customized textbook within days. This has created an environment of decentralized and dynamic versions of what used to be a library delivery function. The value-added difference for users is that they can keep up with rapid changes in their fields while putting a personal imprimatur on course outlines and reading lists.

What we now have is an environment where the raw materials in library collections are being used in dynamic ways to create new customized information sources and services. Copying stores are turning into publishers and bookstores. Bookstores are turning into publishers, and publishers are beginning to offer text-delivery services from their own databases in order to compete with commercial copy operations and with libraries. In this setting, the age-old business relationships between publishers and the information providers can go in two directions: their long history and experience in offering facsimile services can be solidified; or the information industry can collaborate to develop delivery systems that virtually bypass information centers and leave them with a passive role.

Just as there are wrenching changes (and hard decisions to make) about how best to spread a little money a long way in staffing and providing materials within information centers, so are there similarly dramatic changes occurring in access and delivery systems. While some of these issues and future changes are explored further in Chapter 8 – particularly from the point of view of the role of the library's ability to provide access to information outside of its own walls – we would be remiss if we did not next address one of the primary forces of change, the information technologies. In the next chapter, information systems and services are viewed from the technological perspective, information services as at once becoming easier to use and harder to understand.

5 Information technologies

- ◆ Basic choices
- ◆ Turnkey solutions
- ◆ Buying or leasing software
- ◆ Installed databases
- ◆ Imaging
- ◆ Legal issues
- ◆ Future strategies

Until recently, information technology in libraries and information centers was used mostly to automate their internal operations, such as lending, ordering, cataloging, and interlibrary loan. Now the information systems and attendant technologies tend to be viewed as integral parts of an organization's infrastructure. Whether the information system and supporting technologies operate as an independent entity or as part of a wider integrated information system supporting the entire organization, matters not for purpose of this review. Focus in this chapter is on the capacities and decisions about the technologies as they affect the information service and delivery of information.

❝ The very nature of the information service function – and the technology infrastructure which supports it – are changing far more rapidly than the ability and or desire of most libraries to implement new services. The needs are clear; the gap between service demands and budgets is growing. Outsourcing is not a panacea. However, it should be evaluated as a cost and service improvements for those areas which do not directly affect the library's ability to fulfill its mission. In addition, the outsourcing evaluation process is likely to highlight areas for improvement, with or without the move to outsourcing. So, why not evaluate it?

The entire world system of information service providers is facing increased pressure to become more competitive in virtually every aspect of its delivery of services. More information is being created, stored and shared. And, more *people are accessing the same information in different locations, at different hours, and for different purposes.*

Complicating this environment of information implosion is the ever-increasing rate of technological evolution. New technologies have provided for more cost-effective, but not always complementary, models of computing.

In addition, budgets are down and service demands are up. To meet these challenges, libraries need to find ways to make their information technology do more, do it better, and do it for less. **"**

Carole Cotton

◆ Basic choices

Information service organizations have three basic hardware choices when they want to automate: a mainframe or mini-computer configuration, a microcomputer-based (usually with a hard disk) system, or a CD-ROM based set-up. Generally, decisions about the final configuration are based on the size of the organization, its population of users, and factors like the number of prospective simultaneous transactions anticipated on the system. If the organization is contemplating a total information system, the most appropriate configuration will become quite obvious. For example, a CD-ROM based option would rarely be used if the information system is projected to need online operation of all traditional library-related operations, access to online commercial databases and electronic publications, links to other local information systems, image databases, electronic delivery of documents, and connections with other telecommunication networks and services. In other words, for this kind of comprehensive application, mini- and main-frame options are most likely to provide the needed capacity.

Similarly, the need to handle multiple functions for a large number of simultaneous users points to the upper end of systems. The usual patterns for supplying the requisite amount of mainframe computing for information systems has been to either use an existing under-utilized mainframe, or to buy or lease a dedicated machine. In the early days of automation of libraries, information systems often shared equipment that was purchased or leased cooperatively by a group of institutions. This option was mostly driven by the fact that only with combined buying power could the partners afford what was needed. If an information center wants to automate only a limited number of functions such as an online catalog of its holdings, then a CD-ROM set-up may suffice. While the low-end microcomputers and CD players needed to operate such a set-up are relatively inexpensive, and these systems can be outsourced, the cost to produce the first master CD can be prohibitive, particularly if the organization is producing its own disks. Response time is generally good, and cataloging data updates for such an online catalog can be provided by some book vendors. The CD-ROM catalog option is best suited for smaller limited service operations, where frequent updates are not required, even though some larger libraries do use networks of CD-ROMs to augment mainframe systems. If CD-ROM data disk products are used on networks, vendors may place limitations on the size of the network or charge license fees for network use. Some, for example, will permit network use only if the CD-ROM products are used in one location and not on organization-wide networks.

Microcomputer-based systems that use hard disks and local area networks to link two or more workstations are popular choices in many small to medium sized libraries. These systems are a growing market since it is the smaller information centers that tend to remain unautomated today. Some PC-based systems, when used in conjunction with a local area network and/or a CD-ROM servers, can rival mini- and main-frame systems in both function and capacity. This market is now being eyed by vendors who previously concentrated on upper-end applications. For these reasons, applications that operate on upper-end microcomputers may become ever viable options for a number of information centers, particularly since prices are affordable, ranging from less than US$1 000.00 to US$10 000.00.

" Universities in general and leading-edge institutions in particular tend to be quick to embrace new technology and offer new services. Unfortunately, the remaining 3 200 schools lag far behind them in offering new services. A recent study on information systems in higher education highlights the following:
1. Only 22 per cent of the libraries are connected to the campus backbone;

2. *Only 11 per cent reported campus-wide access to index and/or abstract services;*
3. *Fewer than 50 per cent of the schools reported network access to one or more outside libraries and*
4. *Only 21 per cent reported having plans to implement OSI-compliant (Z39.50) protocols which would permit one library system to access bibliographic data on another library system.* **"**

Carole Cotton

Most organizations (academic, public, school, commercial, industrial, etc.) are now interested in information systems that can handle multiple functions and multimedia, are open-ended, and provide network access. Needs are currently well beyond basic internal functionality. The tendency now is to demand a high degree of flexibility in providing customized enhancements, as well as gateways to other local sources of information and to external information sources. From the earliest days of automation of libraries, a great deal of emphasis was placed on the development of systems that meet local parameters. As a result there were developed a number of dynamic yet functionally stable systems available to purchase or lease, or for use through collaborative arrangements some of which are still on the market.[1]

Ideally, information access and retrieval systems and their attendant hardware should be selected with the productivity of the end-user as the primary concern.

" *This is most important – and radical. One of the most difficult problems facing systems developers and marketers for the library market is that the buyers of these systems are not usually the end users of the systems, and further also have different and sometimes conflicting requirements from the end-users.*

This has led to a tremendous concentration on the perfection and nearly infinite customization of the 'back room' support subsystems such as bibliographic maintenance, serials control, circulation control and the like, and to considerably less attention paid to the primary end-user

---

[1] Fayen (1983), Matthews (1986), Potter (1986), Reynolds (1985) and issues of *Library Technology Reports* provide good descriptions of these systems and their applications.

interfaces and capabilities in public access catalogs. It is demonstrably the case that a library systems vendor, with say $100 000 to spend on enhancement and development of something, will realize far more immediate gain (sales) by glitzing up the bibliographic cataloging module to give some efficiency or new capability to the back room than by working on the development of new capabilities for the public catalog end-users. Indeed, many of the capabilities requested by the marketplace even for public catalogs are oriented to highly specialized and probably librarian-oriented activities instead of toward support of end users. A typical request for proposal (or information) for a library system will contain less than 10 per cent of the requirement oriented to the public catalog, and 80–90 per cent to extraordinary detail of specification for back room systems, along with details of why this library's requirements are different from every other library's requirements for the same tasks. **"**

Ward Shaw

In fact, information technology is generally selected first on the basis of what is affordable and secondly on compatibility with the rest of the organization. Nevertheless, if customer satisfaction is considered, Epstein (1991) suggests that the following functions be available:

- catalogs that can include all material types, not just the books;
- leads that point the user to pamphlet files and informs the user of other uncataloged and ephemeral materials;
- inclusion of automated community information files and files that provide information on the contents of journals;
- an accurate system of cross-references that takes the user from his/her search terms to the terminology used by the organization;
- the ability to find non-roman character materials, including foreign subject headings.

An increasingly important capability is connectivity – the ability to accept files of information (about users, books, text data) from other systems and to provide seamless connections for users to either the wider organizational network and/or to external networks. In other words, as the basics of information systems to automate internal operations have been put in place, more sophisticated messages about more outward-looking expectations are being sent to vendors for future enhancements. Information systems usually aim to streamline operations and to provide more cost-effective service. While decisions about information technology applications have to be realistic, ideally they should have as foremost the goal of high quality service decisions rather than expedience and affordability. This is easy to say and hard to do in a climate that sees such rapid change in not just hardware and software but also in user expectations.

❝ During the 1980s it was true that information technology could be viewed as a series of alternatives, such as turnkey versus software only, and centralized information databases versus locally mounted files. Institutions chose the alternatives to best fit their budget or expertise. Such clearcut decisions are no longer possible. The offerings of the 1980s, regardless of form, have raised user expectations. Those expectations can no longer be met with one type of information technology.

A major factor in creating these increased expectations has been the success of automating the 'finding' records for library collections – the online catalog. Once these 'finding' records became available, users came to believe that all types of information were available online. This is exemplified by the frequent tales of librarians trying to deal with users' confusion over the content of CD-ROM databases versus online catalogs. The viable organization must now provide it all.

Another element of increased expectations is the more powerful personal computer. End-users are bombarded in the media with images of very powerful devices that graphically provide information. It is impossible for the average person to understand that the creation of a single graph from a small set of numerical data is very different to the delivery of census or scientific data. Because the end-user believes that the end-user workstation is the ultimate delivery vehicle, the organization is again faced with the need to both provide the workstation and fulfill the expectations. ❞

Jane Burke

Traditionally, computer engineers, managers and support personnel have been perceived by many as being out of touch with users' computing needs, and as having a technology fixation. Librarians and other information professionals have tended to be tarred with the same brush, although they have a history of practical experience in interpreting users' needs and have tried to develop local systems using technologies from the commercial sector. Combined, the two worlds have in many cases succeeded in designing systems that automate 'what is' rather than what should be. They have, for example, succeeded in creating online catalogs that are perfect emulations of the infamous 3 in × 5 in cards and can be used in the same serial fashion.

Although it has taken over 20 years to reach the current state, a growing number of information professionals are finally re-examining old premises about 'automation' and exploring the outer boundaries of the capacities of the information technologies. Hypertext and expert systems are being tested in collaboration with software and hardware vendors to develop the next generation of information access and retrieval systems. Although not yet a stampede, there are signs that De Gennaro's 1985 prediction is coming true. He said that: 'In the next decade, the creative development work will no longer be limited to the small entrepreneurial vendors as it has been in recent years. They will be joined by the systems groups that are now being reconstituted and revitalized in many libraries after a decade of relative inactivity and decline. The work of this new generation of systems librarians will be augmented and supplemented by the efforts of a growing army of the enthusiastic volunteers drawn from the rank and file of the professional staff' (De Gennaro, 1985, p. 40).

While systems are evolving, choosing a system, be it basic or an enhanced information access and retrieval system, requires techni-cal in-house expertise as well as knowledge about the way in which these systems can be acquired.

" *The information technology model of the 1990s has the following characteristics:*
1. *client/server model*
2. *distributed hardware and software*
3. *joint efforts between institutions and vendors*
4. *tiered information files*

1. Client/server model

This means that the software (the client) used by the end user is separate from the data being accessed. It is designed to provide for very easy use, including graphics and windows and allows for the display of a variety of kinds of data.

Each file is stored in the manner appropriate to the data, utilizing hardware and software that will vary from file to file (the server). A simplistic client/server model for libraries and information organizations consists of four components:

End User	Information intermediary
Client	Client
Information database	Transaction database
Server	Server

Thus, the automated information system includes workstations for users, different workstations for library staff and a variety of databases including citations, full text, images, and acquisition, fund accounting, and circulation records.

2. Distributed hardware and software

Different hardware and software are blended together in an inherently distributed manner to use the most efficient and cost-effective pieces for each requirement. Thus, the major information databases might reside on a fast machine, while less used files utilize a CD-ROM jukebox that has been attached to the network. Library staff may continue to use 386 machines while some end-users invest in image display devices.

3. Joint effort

No single institution or vendor is able to build all of the components of this information system of the 1990s. Equally important, no single organization can maintain, document, and constantly enhance such a system. The provision of information to end-users requires strong partnerships between local staff and vendors. The role of local staff is to do (or to hire) systems integration. Less application, but more networking knowledge is required of the institution.

4. Tiered information files

The information files accessed by users do not reside in any one location. Highly used files, such as the online catalog and certain journal citation databases, are mounted locally. Other lesser used or larger files are shared among several institutions. Still others are mounted on a central utility. The software used in the information system makes these tiers virtually invisible to users. The charges, if any, for the data are tabulated automatically and appear on some sort of administrative report, such as a telephone bill. **"**

Jane Burke

◆ Turnkey solutions

If little in-house expertise is available, purchase or lease of a 'turnkey' or 'off-the-shelf' system may be the best choice. This type of purchase is relatively simple and implementation is about as uncomplicated as it can get. The qualifiers are intentional since purchase of turnkey systems can easily become complicated, particularly if the system selection is not based on an appropriate set of criteria.

Turnkey systems generally come packaged with full documentation, hardware, disk drives, tape drives, operating system licenses, telecommunications equipment, software, and peripheral equipment such as barcode scanners, printers, and terminals, etc. Vendors will handle installation (including loading databases), staff training, migration of services from the old system to the new system, and will provide a maintenance agreement.

If outsourced, a turnkey information system will relieve an organization of responsibility for financing the system and for performance guarantees. These risks are borne by the contractor who assumes full responsibility for failure of the system, regardless of the cause. Since the vendor determines the organization's hardware needs, purchases the hardware, and warrants its performance, the information center is relieved of the responsibility to finance the hardware purchase. Finally, many turnkey system contracts are performance-based, wherein a percentage of the initial price is withheld by the purchasing organization until the entire system is up and running in an operating mode. While this means that the information center is not responsible for any system-implementation failure costs, it also means that it gets the blame for problems but cannot fix them directly.

The decision to buy or lease something other than a turnkey system therefore rests largely on whether the appropriate staff and resources are available to calculate the necessary system configuration, negotiate for the various pieces of the configuration, and configure and implement the system, and whether the needed financial resources are available to assume the burden of financing the startup costs for hardware and software. If most of these elements are not in place, then a turnkey solution is probably most appropriate.

◆ Buying or leasing software

If an organization has computing capacity that is under-utilized, purchase or lease of applications software is sometimes a truly viable option. Again expertise will be needed to calculate the capacity needed in both the software and the hardware. Although some vendors will do this, it is preferable to use internal or external consultants. As with turnkey systems, some vendors will do the entire installation, but software vendors are more likely to expect that the information center will have in-house expertise to help configure, install and maintain the system once it is operating.

The software-only option has distinct economical advantages if other circumstances are right. The right circumstances would have to include: the already-owned equipment is new and well maintained; the appropriate compatible operating systems are available or can be added; the costs to maintain it are shared equitably; performance guarantees are provided; guarantees on the availability of system resources are provided; and the hardware can be upgraded to accommodate future growth. Then purchase or lease of just applications software is a safe choice. Normally installation of a leased or purchased information access and retrieval software on existing hardware will entail some sort of service agreement between the information center and the computing center, even if only informally. In this kind of operation, the hardware and at least parts of the software operations are being outsourced.[2]

If the needed hardware and network systems are not available in-house, procurement arrangements with a vendor may also be an economical solution. There could be benefit from sizable manufacturer discounts but some risks are associated with calculating the necessary equipment configuration. Since the software vendor is not usually involved in the sale of the hardware, the cost of the software (including future upgrades) may be adjusted to decrease credits otherwise assumed in a turnkey-type purchase. And, while hardware manufacturers' discounts can be very attractive, organizations should be aware that some manufacturers have different discounts on a type-of-organization basis, e.g. academic vs. public sector, and commercial vs. industrial.

If the organization does not own hardware, it could also consider a hardware lease option. Viviano (1984) stated that the use of leased equipment has several benefits. As with the turnkey system option, hardware leasing is a hedge against technological obsolescence, it allows the lessee to transfer tax benefits associated with ownership to the lessor, it allows better asset utilization, 100 per cent financing, avoidance of capital budget constraints, and it facilitates equipment upgrades. Viviano also provides a guide to choosing a leasing company, and suggests careful consideration of this option based on the value of the equipment and the value associated with acquiring its use.

Once the decision has been made to purchase or lease the hardware associated with a software-only procurement, the organization can assume that it will receive at least the following with the software contract:

1. Full documentation on the system and its subsystems;
2. Installation of the software;
3. Database loading services;
4. Migration services from the old system to the new system;
5. Some training of the local systems staff;
6. Software warranty agreement; and
7. Software maintenance and upgrade agreement.

---

[2] See Woodsworth and Williams (1988) for a description of the elements of system support agreements in situations where a library or information center 'contracts' for operation of its systems to another unit in the organization.

As mentioned previously, a decision to acquire only applications software also assumes that the purchasing organization has, or has access to, an excellent applications and systems staff. They are needed to train other staff, write interface software, design screens, perform database upgrades, set up database security and staff authorization levels to use various functions of the system, prepare database indexing specifications, arrange for downloading and uploading agreements with external utilities, provide problem resolution and quality assurance on the existing system and its upgrades, act as a liaison between the various administrative units of the organization, engage in systems planning (including budgeting for systems applications and operations), participate in negotiations with vendors on the procurement, installation, operation and evaluation of peripheral equipment, provide technical consultation on new databases, new systems, and system growth, and sometimes maintain the telecommunications system on which the automated system runs. In short, this option needs resident information professionals who can adapt the software to the local information center's operations and services.

Some information centers, as has been mentioned earlier, can only manage to use the information technologies if they are purchased or leased jointly with others. Among the 'costs' of such consortia arrangements is that some local parameters may have to be altered to meet group standards, and selection, installation, and enhancements may be slower than would be expected in a single site installation. Regardless of the type of system an organization chooses to purchase, consortia arrangements with other institutions lead to a long roster of issues that are affected. If such arrangements are anticipated, Walton's (1990) checklist of issues associated with shared automated systems governance is worthwhile consulting.

◆ Installed databases

As alluded to in Chapter 4, in addition to being available in print and on CD-ROM disks, many organizations choose to mount citation and whole text databases locally and make them widely available through the organization's network. The installation of these electronic products in the information system usually requires a lease or site license arrangement with the vendor and/or database producer. The decision to install a database on a mainframe system and to provide network access to it versus having disk or CD-ROM access within a distinct service area is not a light one from a fiscal point of view. The cost can increase a hundredfold with an organization-wide site license.

In either case, the resulting license can be restrictive and the decision to provide this type of broad access via the mainframe should take into account the nature and size of the user group as well as the subject areas to be covered (with attention to whether there is a local collection of supporting materials, the strength of that collection, and current investments in those subject areas). The cost of the database compared to existing access methods and anticipated use needs to be analyzed along with the ease of access to the database, and the means to limit that access to the specified user group. As with CD-ROM 'lease' agreements, this type of license agreement will likely have to be reviewed and approved by those responsible for computer license agreements and/or the legal staff of the institution.

Like CD-ROM products, loading commercial database on a local mainframe can provide a value-added option to inferior and dated print resources. Unlike CD-ROM products, however, these data-bases can provide economies of scale by enabling access to a far larger number of simultaneous users. In other words, if one considers the number of simultaneous uses, the time-saving advantages of much quicker search software, the organization's current investment in the subject area (if any), then the added value of convenient access, leasing and loading tapes may prove to be more cost-effective than the lease of the same product in CD-ROM format. This is particularly so if the organization can share the cost of the lease in a consortium arrangement with other organizations. If a cost benefit analysis process proves otherwise, then the organization will be able to lease several CD products with the dollars it would have spent on one tape product.

◆ Imaging

The future use of imaging technology for high-speed, economical and customized print-on-demand services also portends yet more leasing arrangements for information service organizations. Com-panies like Canon, Kodak, IBM, and Xerox are already releasing imaging products, and it appears that they will offer significant service and space-saving advantages to the information services community. To date, the application of advanced digital scanning, data management and printing technologies to the storage and delivery of information materials exists in only a few pilot projects. The commercial publishing sector, however, has already recognized the business advantage of creating, producing and distributing some products only in electronic format. With a little more investment in research and development of the imaging technologies, the information services and publishing communities will be challenged not only to apply this technology to local information delivery operations, but also to move it into network environments in support of the production, distribution, archiving, preservation and access to information.

In this emerging environment, it is likely that information services centers will lease imaging equipment and workstations for local storage and for access to and delivery of a growing number of 'leased', high-use core materials. At the same time, they will depend on the infrastructure for network-based publishing for access to non-core, copyright-cleared, and infrequently used material through a pay per copy, access service fee, subscription, or other similar payment arrangement. Imaging technology can significantly change the archival and retrieval functions of many organizations for certain kinds of materials, particularly in an access-based paradigm.

Information workstations

Another forceful development in the information technologies is the empowered individual information workstation. These operate on high-end microcomputers with the capacity to communicate over high-speed networks both locally and globally. Prototypes are being developed that are capable of bringing information to the user when and where it is needed, with the necessary power and programs to apply the information retrieved to the specific user needs. Those needs include word processing, integration of full-text files available locally and at other institutions with original data sets, access to local and other automated catalogs, use of local and other digitized collections of pictures, maps, graphs, etc., access to bulletin boards and mail files, keyword access to local and other bibliographic databases, access to optical disks stored locally and elsewhere, and the ability to save the results of searches.

While information service professionals are slowly realizing the profound implications of these workstations, they have not taken the lead in structuring the tools and services that will accommodate the variety of potential needs of a given user at his/her workstation. There is no doubt that this type of advanced computer will eventually become a basic piece of equipment for professionals, scholars and researchers. The cloudy question is how they will fit with information service operations. If they are developed and controlled by information centers, they might best be treated as leased and not owned commodities, given their dynamic nature. If they are developed and marketed by the private sector, information service centers may be left to figure out how they can assist and link with these powerful workstations. Irrespective of their eventual domain, powerful information workstations are still among the emerging technologies. To make them real and reachable on a mass level, much work is still needed by information service professionals and software and hardware wizards on operating system consistency, data exchange standards, a consistent user interface, and useful (simple) networking protocols. From the financial perspective, information service center budgets and the budgets of information systems vendors will need to include resources that can fully develop these and other experimental information technologies.

❝ The real challenge for the development and implementation of library systems is to directly confront the exploding panoply of information sources and avenues through emerging networks, and to somehow make that accessible, controllable, and useful to the end-user, wherever he or she may be. No one knows how to do this, and our only hope of useful approach is through new partnerships and collaborations in which different players with different kinds of expertise return to their respective first principles, concentrating on what they best bring to a solution that by its nature is larger than any individual institution, single profession, or market segment.

Another challenge is for professionals to participate in and contribute to the larger professional world, thus bringing that world back to their local environment, and not in the name of

*economy return their efforts and focus exclusively to their
local setting. Further, these activities must be supported. This
seems contradictory, and will certainly invite challenge from
the bean counters. So be it. Those challenges must be met,
otherwise our systems will be poorer, our standards restrictive
instead of enabling, and our users doomed to decreasing
access to more and more confusion. And, in the end, the bean
counters will have a lot more beans to count if we succeed.* **"**

Ward Shaw

◆ Legal issues

So far we have made much mention of leases, licenses and
contracts. Before concluding this chapter on future strategies for
the information technologies, there are some legal concerns that
managers must appreciate.

As with any contractual arrangements, it is standard operating
procedure in buying or leasing an information system to prepare
technical specifications. These outline the organization's needs,
sometimes in agonizing and unrealistic detail.

The specifications document sometimes includes a cover
memorandum that outlines the expectation of both parties regard-
ing procedures and practices and their intent to strike an effective
balance between the organization's needs and the vendor's
products and services. Usually included in the memorandum of
understanding are statements related to annual audits of the
vendor's accounts, financial stability, software, hardware capacity
and growth, long-term hardware plans, operational plans and
development priorities of the vendor, the vendor's disaster
recovery plan and alternate computer site, back-up data storage
arrangements, and the organization's ability to participate in the
setting of software development priorities.

The memorandum of understanding and the technical specifications normally form the basis of the contract between the
organization and the vendor. The contract in turn usually
addresses performance and functionality provisions, specifications
and timetables for implementation of existing systems/subsystems,
as well as those under development, management reports from the

vendor to the organization, telecommunications specifications, and a payment schedule (preferably performance-based).

The bidding process for information systems is not much different than bidding process for new carpeting in an office area. However, since information systems are more dynamic than carpeting, the trend is to issue an RFI (Request for Information) rather than the more rigid RFP (Request for Proposal). The former leaves more latitude for issuers and respondents to interact creatively and to alter specifications and terms of acceptance. For example, if an information software vendor has created a feature that the information center had not envisioned, an RFI would enable both to discuss and bargain over the value of the enhancement.

Another difference between normal contracts for services or products in the information industry is that performance measures are difficult to define and, if defined, hard to enforce. Therefore, management must exercise more discretion in both purchase and leasing contracts than is the case with other things such as equipment without a human service component – e.g. photo-copiers.

A final complication in the information technology world is that client–vendor contracts inevitably entail a long-term relationship. There are a limited number of information technology hardware and software vendors. Lack of standardization means that it is not at all easy to change from one vendor or system to another. Thus, before an organization says 'I do' to an IT vendor, both must find their values and policies at least acceptable if not compatible.

◆ Future strategies

The last chapter in this book deals with changes in the services, roles, and funding structures of information centers. As a backdrop to that discussion, concepts such as a 'library without walls' and the 'electronic library' merit space here.

These terms generally refer to the changes that traditional libraries have been experiencing, and will continue to undergo well into the next century. Some libraries may never reach states that merit those names. When, however, the information pro-fessions talk about the future of the library as being without walls, or electronic, there are some commonly understood assumptions about that future.

It is generally accepted that the electronic information center will include paper and museum artifacts, along with materials in electronic format. It is envisioned that they will offer the means to identify, locate, and request material from various local and remote collections. In other words, the components of the traditional library will be merged with the components of other electronic information sources. These components will include many of the resources and technologies that are discussed throughout this book: the citations, entire texts, numeric, statistical, and image databases, journal indexes and abstracts, electronic publications, network-based information resources, etc. It is also agreed that these will be available through the use of such services as electronic document retrieval and delivery. These 'electronic libraries' will probably run fully or partially leased technologies (software, computing equipment, telecommunications lines, etc.), and will be embedded in an international computing and tele-communications infrastructure. The new technologies associated with imaging, print-on-demand and network-based information resources will expand the scope and coverage of traditional information services and resources, while merging the boundaries between computing services, libraries, data archives, museums, and the commercial/non-commercial information industry.

'Electronic libraries' will probably develop incrementally from today's information systems that are involved with the Internet. They could however go leap-frogging into the future and overturn all of today's premises about information transfer – as did the automobile and television when they were introduced. Whatever we cannot predict, it is fairly safe to say that, for some time to come, information professionals will only provide their users with information about the resources located at their own site, or those that they are knowledgeable enough to make accessible through collections of databases, computing systems, and network-based document delivery services.

One of the most intriguing and forward-looking studies on the electronic library is a development plan created by Sirbu (1991) and a group of graduate students at the Information Networking Institute, a joint venture between Carnegie Mellon University, Bellcore, and the Regional Bell Operating Companies. They proposed a plan for a large publisher to test the operability of a nationwide distributed electronic library system. It included a market test plan, a technical blueprint of the system architecture, and economic models for a national market test. The focus of this plan was to create an environment where the workstation becomes the library, with all electronically published information stored at central servers, and accessible through telecommunications networks. This is by far the most comprehensive model available today on the development of an electronic library whose services could be provided on a pay-per-use basis.

The 'electronic library' could also be created through other outsourcing models, including national site license arrangements with publishers, or print-on-demand services from publishers, bookstores, other third parties, etc. Whatever the model, it is apparent that automated information system vendors will be competing in a marketplace that is substantially driven by the private sector and network limitations. Peters (1991) has described the mandates for simplification, connectivity and performance in that environment. In a marketplace where leasing information technology, not ownership, is the future norm, it is obvious that the competitive design of future automated information systems will have to be based on these same three mandates.

Much the same view is presented by West and Katz (1990, p. 33). They describe a viable information infrastructure as consisting of five elements:

- networking
- information resources
- access and processing tools
- document delivery capabilities
- user support

They also call for a major shift in the vision and strategies for both the development and financing of a network-based information exchange medium, and outline three investment principles that are needed to guide this vision (p. 34):

1. Institutional investments should be based first on their potential to increase institutional productivity;
2. Investments should be based on the leverage potential of the investment; and
3. Investments should emphasize lowering support costs.

The critical point in their argument is that institutions should have a long-term investment strategy for information technology, including an identification of targeted investment areas, and an eye for the investment partners to achieve the vision. While their article is focused on the academic computing environment, these principles are applicable in all environments that are planning to move beyond their present level of use of information access and retrieval systems.

The need to invest wisely in the information technologies is clear. Whether to do so through ownership or outsourcing is less clear and each organization makes important and lasting choices when they determine what information power to acquire and how to sustain that power. In making those decisions, the roles of collaboration and joint ventures are as important as Ascher's (1987) reasons for outsourcing: cost-effectiveness, lack of in-house expertise, the need to reduce overhead, greater administrative convenience, and the need for increased flexibility to respond to changes in market conditions.

" *Outsourcing should be considered when any of the following conditions exist:*

- *when information technology expenses are growing faster than budgets;*
- *when demand for the quantity and quality of services outstrips an organization's ability to provide them;*
- *when the skills to evaluate, implement, and manage new technologies do not exist;*
- *when the time and energy devoted to managing information technology interferes with its ability to focus on the central mission of the library.*

Which aspects of information technology should be considered for outsourcing? The answer lies in identifying those elements of information technology which generally support two functional needs: core competencies and 'utility' functions. Core competencies and the information technologies which directly support them are strategic to the central mission of the organization and should be maintained in-house. In contrast, technology-based utility functions should be treated like other classes of utilities such as heat, light, and telephone service, and individually evaluated as candidates for outsourcing.

Core library competencies include those activities which support the ability to acquire, archive, access/retrieve and deliver information services. At a minimum, the technical expertise to define, evaluate and customize the applications software and the user interface, whether developed in-house or purchased externally, must be maintained within the library. In contrast, 'utility' functions are not strategic to the mission of the library. While they must be executed well, they represent generally available, commodity based skills and thus are candidates for outsourcing. A few typical examples follow:

1. System operation and ownership
2. System level development
3. Network implementation and management
4. Back-office operations like payroll, billing, accounts payable, etc.

Once functions are identified as candidates for outsourcing, the evaluation should include consideration of at least the following:

1. Short and long-term financial implications
2. Transition plans
3. Personnel impact
4. Cultural impact
5. Security
6. Loss of control
7. Vendor performance record

In summary, outsourcing is not the right solution for all information service providers – or even for all information technology functions within an institution. In particular, core competencies should never be outsourced. But, given a forecast of continued downward pressure on budgets and upward pressure on service demands, the issue must be raised – of whether to outsource or not. The question may be more important than the answer. **"**

Carole Cotton

The key question for those who are casting a cold eye on information systems and information technologies is: 'Should we spend the resources to create and maintain an in-house capacity, or should we shift that cost (or part of that cost) to an external source?' Outsourcing the functions, activities and associated information technology described in this chapter is an economically viable option. Like any other choice, it carries some risks. Perhaps the greatest risk is not making a choice at all – or, in today's volatile climate of change and uncertainty, choosing to stay with yesterday's mission and values.

" Use of external sources of tools (hardware and software) and data is essential to fulfilling the end users' expectations in the 1990s. The profit motivation drives the development of the variety of sources necessary.

The role of the local information manager is one of choosing the best sources from among alternatives. "

Jane Burke

6

Shared or cooperative routes

◆ Reasons for sharing
◆ Pooling information resources
◆ Public information highways
◆ Paying for collaboration
◆ The down side

❝ There are more reasons to turn to inter-institutional information resource sharing these days than there were when the present cooperatives were being organized less than 20 years ago. First, libraries have had such success with resource sharing in the areas of bibliographic control and interlibrary lending that there is a natural tendency to turn towards cooperation as a means of solving other information difficulties. If it worked once, let's try it again. Second, it is apparent that individual libraries cannot solve alone the information crisis and fiscal problems which are so overwhelming and which so transcend the local scene.

What libraries generally still fail to see, however, is that the solutions to the present problems will require somewhat different models of technological, economic and cooperative resource sharing than those which have served them so well in the recent past. It is no longer going to be business as usual – not even in long-standing library cooperative ventures. **❞**

Harold Billings

When gasoline prices rise, car-pools and public transportation become more attractive to commuters. While individuals save money, they have to put up with some inconveniences. So it is with information services. When expenditures for information resources and services overpower affordability, the option of sharing the cost burden with others becomes attractive. There are many information systems and sources that have been developed for cost avoidance purposes. Cooperatively built repositories of information and cooperatively managed electronic networks to connect them have had some historical success, particularly in North America. Before organizations decide to abandon their local library and information centers in favor of reliance on shared or cooperative centers, it behoves them to understand and appreciate the problems and pitfalls that come with this alternative.

◆ Reasons for sharing

" It is hard to quantify, but ours is a networking profession. We see cooperation as one of our most important shared values. "

Kenneth E. Dowlin

The information professions have a long history of cooperation in delivery of their services. Since their purpose is to make information accessible, their instinct to cross institutional boundaries simply reflects a professional value. There are other more tangible reasons, however, for resource-sharing.

Fiscal constraint and the resulting need to save money by pooling resources are certainly primary motivators. In the early days of automation of libraries, for example, hardware costs were prohibitive for individual institutions. Alliances of libraries of the same type, or those in close geographic proximity, were often begun to enable the shared purchase and use of hardware and applications software to support information operations. Although this kind of cost-sharing has been common, it has had the added benefit of enabling more to be done more effectively. It did not always eliminate or reduce operating costs.

Another argument used to justify participating in joint/shared projects is the ability to get enhanced capacity and to give better service for marginal increases in cost. Another reason cited is the potential for increased efficiency. For example, a reduction in the amount of time spent locally on tasks that have been done by others in the consortium is often cited as a benefit that outweighs the cash outlay for membership. Finally, within any community of professions, there is always an element of wanting to have the status of 'belonging to the club', if a coalition is perceived to be prestigious.

" One of the most productive reasons for resource-sharing is staff expertise. This becomes even more important as libraries struggle with cultural sensitivity and languages as well as with traditional subject knowledge. Certain activities require a critical mass for efficiency and effectiveness. This was true in the early days of automation when computers were oversized and expensive. Research and development has almost always needed the aggregation of institutions, even if only to pressure vendors into creating systems or to comply with standards. The new challenges that will require cooperation are languages, user-friendly systems, self-help systems, culturally sensitive services, and retrospective conversion of data.

Another reason for cooperation is lobbying, particularly for increased funds. A united front is more effective than one that is disjointed or non-existent. Another factor that argues for cooperation is that the public expects it. Most of the general public do not understand why there are different types of libraries and why they do not work together. Taxpayers assume that they should have access to any library supported by their tax funds.

In addition, cooperative ventures allow leap-frogging of development. Late-comers to the process can catch up with front runners without having to repeat all of the earlier developmental steps. "

Kenneth E. Dowlin

History has identified some known factors in the information services that contribute to the formation, shape and outcomes of inter-institutional cooperation.

1. **Geographical proximity.** Information services and resources that are close together are more likely to assist one another than are two entities that are highly similar but far apart. In the past, it has been easiest to share resources if institutions are readily accessible to one another. The advent of public data communication networks (or information highways as they are sometimes called) is rendering geographical proximity less important.

2. **Availability of start-up funding.** Libraries and information centers usually operate on a shoe-string and are hungry for external funds. If a government agency provides competitive grants for cooperative projects to be established, information

professionals have been known to devise projects that will get them additional funding even if the commitment to resource-sharing is lukewarm.

3. **Past successes and failures** of some members. If one or more of the participants in a group effort have had prior successful experience in a similar venture, the odds of starting a new cooperative enterprise will improve considerably. With too many doubters and dissenters, a project might never see the light of day.

4. **Technological capabilities** to facilitate sharing of information, services and resources. In today's highly developed technological environment, computing and telecommunications systems enable virtually instantaneous digital delivery of information irrespective of its original format – paper, video, audio, etc.

5. **Common interests and goals**. Like minds think alike and get along. Therefore if two independent information service units want to buy a widget transmitter but neither can afford one on their own, they will naturally be tempted to pool their funds and buy one together.

6. **Leadership**. The presence of advocates and visionaries who see the long-term benefits are needed to persuade those whose attitudes are proprietary and locally oriented.

7. **Commitment from the top**. Passengers and back-seat drivers have a hard time controlling a bus without a driver on board. Although this factor is listed last, collaborative efforts are almost guaranteed to fail unless there is conviction and commitment from those in charge of both the library and its parent institution.

The mix and timing of these factors can coalesce to nurture successful cooperative effort or they can work to dissolve existing partnerships. The factors will also, to some extent, define the composition of the group that operates the consortium. The following are generic objectives found in most of the cooperative efforts undertaken by information professionals:

- to strengthen existing resources and library services;
- to facilitate development of access systems and bibliographic control;

- to provide timely and convenient access to and delivery of information;
- coordinate collection development, maintenance, and preservation activities;
- share costs of extraordinarily expensive items which otherwise would be unaffordable; and
- provide opportunities for staff development and management training.

" Three other items that are often found in objectives of a consortium address the needs for participants: to acquire external funding; to increase marketing efforts; and to plan jointly. "

Kenneth E. Dowlin

◆ Pooling information resources

" Technology and cooperation have brought about a remarkable level of bibliographic control on virtually a world-wide basis. Cooperative cataloging programs have reduced library costs, have made library materials more quickly available to the user, and have built massive bibliographic databases for even further resource-sharing. These cooperative efforts are still forcing us to make significant organizational and staffing changes throughout our libraries. The old cataloging order is seeing more para-professional responsibility for cataloging routines, a loosening of formerly fairly rigid (and very costly) national standards, and a move towards machine-assisted processing which will alter long-held organizational patterns and allow the redistribution of library fiscal and human resources for greater effectiveness and efficiencies.

Computer-assisted interlibrary lending programs have also become more successful, supported as they have been by the huge new databases of bibliographic and holdings information constructed and networked through cooperative action. Delivery of information has continued to be the major problem, with the transfer of traditional packages of information – books and journals – still constrained by the limitations of physical delivery mechanisms. Despite *improvements in mail and courier services, traditional interlibrary lending is still a heavily labor-intensive, slow, and less-than-satisfactory means of information sharing. The new technologies, however, offer rapidly developing opportunities for improved information delivery and representation.*

Where libraries and other information agencies once concentrated on the collaborative building of bibliographic databases and resource-sharing systems, it appears to this writer that these agencies must now join in the cooperative development of massive files of electronically imaged or digitally converted full-text information sources. These can be stored in information servers and made available through the thousands of ubiquitous microcomputers dotting the information highways so rapidly threading the electronic landscape. While conversion, storage, and delivery of these files is not cheap, the technology is improving rapidly and the costs are dropping – and, most importantly, will continue to do so. **"**

Harold Billings

The most familiar form of inter-institutional cooperation to the information seekers is interlibrary loan. Obtaining materials from other information centers, if not owned locally, has become a standard way to augment local collections of materials. If the service is provided either free of charge or at a low cost, then it is normally subsidized by external grants of government funding, and thus can become a fairly viable alternative to ownership. For the most part, it was not until recently that the full potential of this kind of resource-sharing became realizable. Until the power of computing was applied to interlibrary loan processes, many hours were spent manually filing information into central 'union cata-logs' in order to know who owned what. Now that data networks provide easy access to thousands of databases and 'union' files around the world, access is seemingly easy. This can be deceiving to the uninitiated, since travelling the networks in search of specific items is much like travelling a network of highways that has no signs and for which no maps exist.

Another problem is that while information about the location of information is more readily found and compiled than ever before, actual delivery of information is not. Traditional library delivery systems, for the most part, still rely on conventional mail or courier to transport physical items. Experiments with delivery of digital information show that the means exist for vast improvements in information delivery. While publishers and the private information sector appear to be poised to capitalize on new kinds of electronic information delivery systems, libraries and individual users have yet to experience its full potential. Until the supporting technologies enter homes and offices and are as pervasive as telephones, traditional library-to-library request and delivery and processing will likely remain unchanged. Thus, while interlibrary lending has become a normal way of doing business in information centers, it still cannot be considered as a substitute for a local collection of information. The local information node is still needed for the foreseeable future.

The database maintained by OCLC is one of the most valuable resources ever developed in support of multiple information retrieval functions. It houses a database built through the collaborative efforts of over 14 000 libraries and information centers around the world. Each member library contributes information about the materials it owns and can search the database for information and resources it needs. The database is the backbone for an international network of lending and borrowing among members. A cooperative and not-for-profit operation, OCLC demonstrates the highest level of potential for pooling information resources through the kinds of activities that are supported by its database.

1. It can provide copies of catalog records to member libraries thereby avoiding the expenses involved in originating those records locally.
2. Members can search the database for the location of materials they want and then request them through an electronic network.
3. Groups of members can create subsets of the database for their region or interest group to facilitate information delivery among a smaller subset of members.
4. Through collective effort, information records that are incomplete or incorrect can be improved dramatically. This improves the odds for success in the search and delivery of information.
5. By providing access to a pool of over 22 million information records members can determine if they want to purchase something already held by other members.

OCLC is not the only such network in the global village, but it is the largest. Others, based in North America, such as the Western Library Network (WLN) and Utlas International, Inc. engage in similar activities, also relying on 'member' contributions to sustain the databases that are at the core of their existence. WLN operates as a not-for-profit, membership-based cooperative while Utlas is an incorporated, private enterprise headquartered in Canada. In many countries, national libraries take on a similar role, maintaining a database of holdings and serving as the switching agent for interlibrary traffic – shunting requests to locations that have the desired items.

The private sector also sells database services both to individuals, organizations and, of course, to libraries, but at present most use of databases comes from libraries and information centers. Until prices are lower, direct sales are unlikely to boom.

" *I would be very surprised to see a significant percentage of the information available on databases become used directly by the consumer in the near future. I think most of the existing database services will find it necessary to use the help of libraries for a long time. Roger Summit of Lockheed often relates that Dialog was intended for the scientist or other end-user. The company has been surprised to find that their best customers are libraries. Dialog realizes very little of their revenue directly from actual consumers.* "

Kenneth E. Dowlin

There are other hurdles to overcome before the information center role as intermediary in database access disappears. The structure of the databases and the commands to carry out successful information searches are too complex for the average individual to use easily and effectively. In addition, although microcomputers with communications capacity are increasingly popular, they have yet to become as pervasive as the telephone either in numbers or in being used as links to information networks.

Other areas that decision-makers often look to as having potential for avoiding local expenditures for information resources are jointly held or shared collections. Why can't we, they say, combine what we have with the library next door and possibly have both of us saving money? Even if we don't save money, could we not have access to a larger pool of resources?

Yes and no are both correct answers to these questions. There are several ways in which responsibility for information resources can be shared.

1. **Designated responsibility**. In such agreements, each participant agrees to assume primary responsibility for a specific type of information or resources that the entire group feels is needed. This is probably the most common form of shared collection development in the history of library cooperation. In the long term, such arrangements can evolve to the point where a local member is putting other parts of their collections at risk (taking more space and budget than can be supported) in order to sustain the subject for which they have cooperative responsibility. There is also the risk that the area originally designated for a given member (and once compatible with its local interest) might not continue to meet local needs after a while.

2. **Joint purchase**. If two or more institutions want something that would be prohibitively expensive for a single one to purchase, they could agree to share the cost and rotate housing and maintenance of the item.

3. **Pooling funds**. In this situation a group of institutions agree to pay $ N per year to purchase and maintain information resources that benefit the group as a whole. One of the most successful of these types of enterprises has been operated by a group of research libraries for nearly half a century. The Center for Research Libraries in Chicago, Illinois, is supported by membership fees and it has built a collection through purchase and deposit of materials by its member libraries.

4. **Negative consultation**. Since some information resources become obsolete (outdated or worn out) and/or prohibitively expensive (such as journal subscriptions), a group can agree to consult before getting rid of the last copy of an item in order to avoid its total loss from the group. Implicit in this kind of arrangement is that the last location to hold an item must be willing to accept indefinite responsibility for maintaining it unless another member of the group takes it on.

5. **Swapmeets**. The exchange of duplicate or unwanted materials at no or low cost has long been a way for information centers to

augment their buying power. Due to staffing constraints in recent years, however, some have phased out labor-intensive operations such as these and have begun to either sell or simply discard their surplus materials. For a time, there was a not-for-profit enterprise headquartered in the US that served as an international clearing-house and redistribution center for surplus books and journals, the United States Book Exchange (USBE). It was disbanded as a cooperative venture after a protracted period of financial difficulty and is now operated by a company.

There have been many creative attempts to minimize local costs such as the above. Few have stood the test of time and even fewer have delivered significant cost savings. Over the past century, delivery systems using saddle-bags, vans, data networks, and telefacsimile transmission have been tested. Some have succeeded in improving access to information. Some have not survived beyond their experimental period.

As with information delivery systems, information professionals have banded together to solve other problems related to their archive function. For example, preservation of information in books, films, microforms, and compact disks have been a long-standing concern among archivists, librarians, records managers and information scientists. Cooperatively-funded and membership-driven conservation and preservation facilities have been established to cope with a problem that transcends individual institutions. Larger research institutions have accepted responsibility for teaching, advising, and assisting smaller information centers with these types of problems. In addition, when space has been in short supply, information centers have sometimes banded together to share rental and maintenance costs of storage facilities. Needless to say, these solutions to collection management problems still cost money but are less expensive than taking unilateral action.

" National and international cooperative action akin to the high level of effort that went into the bibliographic and preservation successes of the past two decades is required. It is especially important that the large amounts of funding and human effort going into preservation help construct a platform for the support of electronic information exchange, not limited to the microfilmed archiving of at-risk library materials.

The use of electronic information sources should also reduce the large, hidden overhead expenses of traditional collections. Most libraries never consider the costs of acquiring, processing, record-keeping, binding, preservation, housing, servicing, and so on, as part of the price paid for subscriptions or monographic holdings. The savings of such operational overheads through electronic information access (which can be expected to decrease in cost) should provide a degree of flexibility to help meet the continuing escalation of costs for traditional materials.

Clearly then, technology and cooperation offer fresh opportunities for an improved bottom line, and cooperative considerations of the information process must lead to a transformation of the economic infrastructure which supports our information needs. How must collaboration itself change?

The organization of cooperation has been in a state of uncertain change the past several years. It still does not at all seem clear that institutions and resource-sharing organizations understand that the comprehensive collection-based library paradigm of the recent past has been changed forever, and that new models of resource-sharing organization and effort must reflect the change. Too many libraries continue to believe they can find a means by which collection comprehensiveness can be maintained just as it was in the past. Too many institutions pursue electronic information delivery systems on an independent basis, without adequate national collaboration or direction. The national and regional networks at their grass roots continue to be too preoccupied with attempting more of the same old solutions for problems which have permuted beyond cure with the common elixirs.

On the other hand, new types of collaboration are also clearly afoot. Libraries are looking beyond other libraries for partners in new cooperative ventures. The enthusiastic joining of effort on behalf of NREN through the Coalition for Networked Information shows that all sorts of institutions are anxious to participate in forward-reaching activities. And this fresh collaboration of groups that seemed to avoid one another in the past also appears healthy – the joining of the library, computing and scholarly communication communities under the CNI umbrella formed by the Association of Research Libraries, CAUSE, and EDUCOM.

Similarly, the Commission on Preservation and Access and the Library of Congress have begun to support imaging and digital text conversion programs among new library consortia. These joint efforts may help carry information systems beyond bibliography and preservation towards a brighter information delivery and presentation future.

In my view, libraries must also join with agencies and firms in the commercial sector in new partnerships to advance the information future. Too much suspicion, competitiveness, and hostility continue to prevail between the public and for-profit camps. OCLC is looking towards such collaboration as it begins action directed towards prospective joint ventures for access and document delivery systems with SilverPlatter and Faxon, as well as its announced joint electronic journal publication venture with the American Association for the Advancement of Science.

There is new interest at the federal level these days in computing, information and electronic highways to carry and join their products, and nothing could promote the collaborative building of broad information systems more than the allure or availability of new government dollars.

What may develop on the European scene as part of the European Economic Community initiatives remains to be determined, but it is obvious that as political and information walls have both tumbled in recent years, neither geography nor other limitation should be allowed to stand between humankind and knowledge. Deeper attention to the opportunities of technology, the careful redistribution of resources throughout the information flow, and new cooperative initiatives can help resolve on a world-sharing basis the present information and fiscal crisis.**

Harold Billings

◆ Public information highways

Roads are most often constructed and maintained by a blend of local, municipal, county, and national governmental funds. If one considers private lanes and driveways to be part of the road system, then private contributions to national and international highway systems become a significant part of our ability to travel from one destination to another. In the electronic information world, there are parallel structures that build, maintain, and develop 'highways' which enable information to move from one site to another.

Companies, schools, or government organizations have built the equivalent of private roads, called local area networks or LANs, mostly to facilitate their internal operations. These LANs can exist independently of each other or they can be connected to one another. If connected, odds are that they are linked through either public, quasi-public, cooperative, or commercially operated networks. An example of a publicly accessible commercial service network is Compuserve. Both individuals and companies can subscribe to this and get access to information services and connections (at least for electronic messaging) to other networks. A consultant in Pittsburgh with access to Compuserve and working on a problem across the Atlantic, can send messages and reports from a home computer through Compuserve to a research institute in Lugano, Switzerland. Be they government operated networks (such as NSFNET or MILNET) research or academic networks (BITNET, EARN, EduNet, MERIT), or private enterprise (TYMNET, Prodigy, Compuserve), leapfrogging between networks is facilitated through a loosely governed network of electronic networks called the Internet.

The research and academic communities have many well developed networks to expedite experiments, communication, and other collaborative work. The library and information science community have also developed networks dedicated to information access and resource sharing. For example, OCLC operates its own telecommunications network that supports connection of libraries and information centers to the central database in Dublin, Ohio. Only libraries, or information processing centers, can access this dedicated network. The Research Libraries Group, with a similar database of bibliographic records in Palo Alto, California, also operates a network dedicated to member access to its central database. Individual libraries can dial up both OCLC and RLG through private network servers such as TYMNET. Individuals can only get access to these multimillion record databases if their institutions provide a gateway to them. Since there are fees for use of databases such as these, organizations naturally have been reluctant to provide individuals with open and uncontrolled access.

In an effort to encourage wider individual use of databases (for a fee) and individual library databases, a growing number of colleges and universities around the world are making their information systems accessible (for free) through the Internet. What this means is that an individual with a modem and a great deal of patience and time can first track down through online (or printed) directories, a list of these freely accessible databases. Then, armed with electronic addresses, instructions for logging in and out on each different system, a patient and dedicated user can find out where certain books, films, music scores, etc. are located – be they from California's university libraries, the University of Maine, or libraries in England, Mexico, or Australia.[1]

While there are some conventions in place that standardize the content of format records in databases, the computer operating systems, the information search strategies, and other user interfaces can differ wildly. Therefore, hunting and pecking through over hundreds of odd library catalogs around the world can be more than a bit frustrating. For this reason alone, libraries will likely continue to maintain union databases such as OCLC's about their resources for some time. Even if there were black boxes between an individual user and remote systems that eliminated system differences and allowed natural language searching across systems, the information professions have a lot of social and policy issues to resolve before global information access becomes as easy as long-distance telephone calls. How, for example, can an individual sitting in St. Boniface, Manitoba, Canada, order and receive a manuscript that is in the Bibliotheque Nationale in Paris? If searching the BN catalog is free via the Internet, what happens with costs associated with transmitting the manuscript? If it is scanned and transmitted as digital signals, who pays for the process of digitizing the item? If the physical object is to be delivered, participating libraries would normally cover the postage costs. If it is not shipped to a library, how would the lender verify the legitimacy of a borrower and impose sanctions against a delinquent borrower? Would libraries accept a credit card deposit as security? How can the person order the item in the first place? Right now, agreements among libraries (called the interlibrary loan

---

[1] Users have to be patient because to date, there is no 'map' or directory that indicates what is available on the 200 000-plus computers on the 346 separate networks that comprise the Internet. For more information see Dalton (1991).

code) would have the St. Boniface public library search for the item first in other Canadian libraries through the National Library of Canada. If not found in Canada, then the National Library would forward the request to Paris. The item would ultimately be sent to the St. Boniface public library, not the individual asking for it.

With direct individual electronic connection now possible, libraries and information centers will have to reconsider the code that dictates that an individual must first travel over all the roads in a country before a border can be crossed. Information providers will also have to reconsider whether, if an individual chooses it, there is to be first-class service. To date, private information vendors have survived because the services they provide are better than those provided free of charge or at little cost by publicly supported information agencies such as libraries. If libraries are to continue to serve as the gateway to information sources beyond the local level, then they will have to consider anew their definitions of basic services and whether or not to offer services and to charge accordingly. In Chapter 8, this complex array of problems is discussed more fully.

From the perspective of decision-makers trying to determine whether their organization is best served with or without access to shared data sources, a number of factors must be considered. Not least among these are the costs of participation.

In Europe, it is common for telecommunications networks to be operated by the government along with telephone and postal systems. In the United States a number of networks were originally funded by and grew out of federal government projects, particularly those dealing with defense, science and technology. There are now many telecommunications networks accessible through complex agreements between countries, agencies, individual institutes and governments.[2] For purposes of information access and delivery their history or even their current names and user populations are unimportant. What is most important is that while this invisible network exists, it is a road little travelled by the average person. To date, only the knowledgeable use the networks and only experts really use them well.

---

[2] John Quarterman's *The Matrix* is a useful compendium of the world's electronic networks. It gives their history, scope and current user configuration (as of 1990).

Simply put, the world-wide networks that comprise the Internet form a daunting maze for most users. As far as providing support to individual workers in search of information to do their jobs, the current telecommunications networks are the equivalent of unmapped mountain trails. They are difficult to find, they take strange and sometimes wonderful twists and turns, they are conducive to getting lost, and they seldom return you to home. As Dalton (1991) points out, there are no maps and only a few guides in training.

At present, telecommunications networks do support data transmission at levels sophisticated enough that the creation of shared information databases is relatively easy despite geographical distances. Standards for formats of data and text, and universally accepted conventions for data communications, have developed sufficiently to allow for exchange of information irrespective of the kind of computer or operating systems being used to transmit information. This is particularly important to the information professions, since information can now be transmitted faster and with less error. When standards for the development of information databases (bibliographic, whole text, images, etc.) and transmission of data have matured sufficiently, a virtual 'library' or the models discussed in Chapters 7 and 8 may become reality. Until then, information seekers will have to live with halting and awkward access to and delivery of information.

The dividends from years of investment in developing large national databases are now being seen. Enhanced local computing and telecommunications capabilities on campus, combined with the large national databases, make it possible for the holdings of remote libraries to be displayed on campus information networks along with the local library 'catalog'. Electronic transmission of bibliographic information, whole text, and research files almost make it possible to eliminate local libraries as we know them today. However, until the technology has provided better delivery mechanisms, age-old questions remain to be answered. If delivery systems are inadequate, what information must be acquired and housed locally? What can we put into remote storage without damaging our ability to retrieve it when needed? How much staff is needed to ensure cost-effective organization and retrieval of information?

Similarly, when the technology is in place to deliver information from remote locations with the same speed and effectiveness as though it were housed at home, another set of questions will have to be asked. For example, as long as delivery systems are adequate, does it really matter where a report or a journal article comes from? The answers may depend on cost. Is it really cheaper for society to be provided with information services by libraries and information centers that do not charge? Or is a mix of private and public information service agencies the most effective approach? Is it more expensive but faster to buy the information from a broker or commercial information service? Apart from social and political questions of equality of access to information, will the levels of service provided be driven by, or drive, the price of getting access?

Similarly, in cooperative ventures, questions of ownership are also important. For example, if retention of historical records is important to an organization, another question may be as follows: If one of a dozen libraries de-acidifies or microfilms a volume to preserve it, and records that information in a shared database, will this mean that some or all of the other libraries still have to preserve the same volume? Logically, the simple answer to this question is 'no'. Emotional responses might differ since, for some, ownership of the work as an artifact can be as important as the information it contains.

◆ Paying for collaboration

" In addition to taking advantage of the new technologies, libraries and the larger information community must make concerted reassessments of the economy of the information flow, from information creation to information consumption. Historically, economic forces have always driven information transfer, providing the environment that has created the production of information machinery, information products, and information consumer markets.

Library managers, however, have generally attacked economic issues in their libraries, or throughout the information flow, with a relative lack of sophistication. A more detailed examination of where resources can be redistributed between creation and use is necessary so that the information community can effect both powerful electronic access and strengthened, distributed collection building.

Libraries have traditionally paid for information access on a sunk-cost basis through the development of local collections. Library users have paid for access to the information in these collections through public taxes, tuition, or other fees that have disguised the fact that the user, or the community on the user's behalf, was paying for access to the knowledge. While cooperative efforts have helped to reduce the rate of rise of costs of information, and induced other savings, the amount of information available and its price will continue to increase beyond any library's capacity to pay for it. And information has to be paid for just like any other commodity.

It is apparent that, in the future, library users will be expected to carry a heavier burden for the payment of access to information – and to information systems which are increasingly value-added. 'Free' access to information has always meant freedom of access to an open system of information and knowledge; it has never meant that users will not ultimately have to pay. It will continue to be a major issue of public policy, at many levels, as to how the community shares the costs of providing information, with special care for the information-deprived.

It is likely that payment for electronic information will increasingly be on a transactional or flat-fee basis, whether by the institution or by the user on a pass-through basis. Libraries will likely pay for a basic level of access for all users; the user will likely pay for more specialized and value-added services. And payment by the user for value-added information system access can free institutional funds to help subsidize the costs of traditional paper-based collections. **"**

Harold Billings

One of the realities of cooperation in the library world is that without external funding, cooperative undertakings seldom start or flourish. Since information services are chronically under-funded, the added costs of cooperative projects can at best carry on as *ad hoc* efforts based on the good will of participants. In fact, lack of funding is often given as a reason for not undertaking cooperative activities at all.

118

Cooperative projects, if they are of a continuing nature need a steady and continuing source of funds. The availability of both start-up and on-going funding is shaky and uneven in most countries. The current economic environment has created a grant climate that is a mixed blessing. While available funds have declined, those that remain are increasingly being awarded to cooperative efforts or projects that demonstrate willingness to build interdependencies among information providers.

At the same time, short-term grants and other 'soft' funds are often provided as seed money to establish coalitions with the expectation that members will bear most of the continuing cost burden of cooperation. In some rare instances, such as in the State of Illinois, the entire operation of ILLINET, including incentives for participating, are being borne by the state government. The Ontario Public Library Information Network in Canada is funded and operated by a branch of the provincial government. Indiana and Nebraska are examples of states that subsidize multi-type library networks heavily. Many of the data networks that form the backbone of the Internet have been funded by the US federal government or a combination of government, private sector and universities.

The costs incurred by being a member of a cooperative information program usually include overheads for a central administration or headquarters. Some smaller joint programs are simply executed by staff from participating organizations. In some instances, such as the regional library networks and OCLC, member contributions plus other sources of income have made them into multimillion dollar operations.

How then do these cooperative enterprises get funds to operate? One obvious source is membership fees. These can either be flat or pro-rated fees (e.g. according to the size of a member's budget, or other measurable factors such as constituency or collection size). In the case of one of the better-known shared research collections, the Center for Research Libraries, member fees are determined by a complex formula that considers factors such as collection size, annual acquisition budget, and the number of branch libraries. Another mechanism for funding joint ventures is to levy a charge for pass-through services. For example, a number of the regional networks that market OCLC products and services add a surcharge to the OCLC bill before sending it to members. These surcharges are sometimes the primary source of revenue for the networks.

Fees for services or products sold is another source of funding for cooperative projects. Sale of services, computing time, consultants, and training, for example, can often more than cover the cost of producing them. Differential fees for members and non-members are not uncommon.

Investment interests and grants from foundations and governments can also be sources of income. The latter tend to be used for special projects and one-time expenditures, since grants do not normally continue indefinitely. Tremendous impetus can be provided by such grants. If, for example, IBM had not supported the creation and formative years of BITNET, it is unlikely that the network would have been established. Finally, some cooperative endeavors, such as individual public sector institutions, recognize that they need to secure a strong base of funding for basic services. To establish this they have turned to fund-raising campaigns to build endowments and/or capital funds.

Among the chronic problems that cooperative projects encounter is how to ensure that the cost burden is distributed fairly among participants. Another recurring problem is the pressure put on members by their constituents to reserve locally supplied budgets for local information services and resources. The benefits of inter-institutional cooperation are not always readily apparent to users, particularly those that enhance 'backroom' operations in libraries, such as cataloging. Similarly, future benefits are hard for users to understand. How, for example, can the importance of a link to the Internet be adequately described when an 'information highway' cannot be touched or seen, or is outside of the experience of most individuals? Returns from investment in cooperative programs are often not immediate. They may, in fact, not yield tangible benefits for years. Worse yet, they are invisible services as far as information seekers are concerned.

In short, it is sometimes difficult to explain and justify real cash expenditures for cooperative ventures. Similarly, the indirect cost of participation in terms of staff time is also a factor that cannot be ignored and must be balanced against the price of membership. With local systems assuming primacy, the cost of maintaining a shared database is being questioned by individual members. To offset real or perceived high costs (actual or perceived), OCLC, for example, restructured its charges to build in better incentives that encourage contributions to maintain the integrity of its database and yet not discourage use of the system. At present, the problem of maintaining the scope of the large bibliographic databases seems, at this time, to boil down to seeing that net contributors are, or at least feel, more fully rewarded.

The biggest problem that all cooperative projects present for information professionals is the lack of comprehensive and rigorous cost studies. Like most efforts at economic analysis of library and information services, current methods are crude. The results of the few studies that have been done provide mixed guidance to decision-makers. Some have concluded that in-house operations provide better quality products and services than would outright purchase from, or participation in, a cooperative group.

A related matter is the extent to which the costs of external services, such as information database access, are absorbed by information agencies or passed onto their users in the form of fees. At present, this question is a direct challenge to the tradition of free library service and equality of access. Some public libraries have tried to control the cost of access to information by limiting direct public access and using librarians as intermediaries. This solution will eventually break down, since many work environments, schools and colleges are leaning toward providing unimpeded direct user access. It is not inconceivable that public pressure will mount for these kinds of services to be available through public libraries.

In the broader context, development of national and inter-national information networks (whether dedicated to information service providers or used by many institutions and organizations), raises serious questions about funding. Within the United States, funding of a National Research and Education Network (NREN) will be a serious challenge for the government to resolve.[3] Its precursor, the Internet, has only indirect government control and a relatively small amount of federal funding but operates relatively well through loose cooperation of participating networks. The Internet has opened up direct access to library databases around the world but, at present, neither the libraries nor the direct users are charged. The connections have been funded by a mix of government funds, donations, membership fees, and direct pay-

---

[3] The US High Performance Computing Act was signed into law as PL102–194 by President Bush on 9 December 1991. The NREN provisions of this law give context and impetus (but without funding so far) for host of networking activities needed to ensure affordable and seamless access to information through high-speed computer-to-computer communication.

ment for services. Although the NREN is envisioned as a public data highway, whether or not it will be operated and funded like a public utility or a for-profit enterprise remains unclear. The potential exists for this type of network, and similar library networks, to charge participants in various ways:

1. Annual or flat fees, like basic telephone service charges;
2. Transaction fees, like toll call charges;
3. Varying fees depending on the type of service used (or the ability to pay; or other graduated payment schemes);
4. Direct or indirect tax-based government subsidy; or
5. Permutations of the above.

Almost all discussions about charges for information bump up against the long-held ethos that library services ought to be funded as a free public good or as institutional overhead and not charged back to individual users. As information services are increasingly delivered over telecommunications networks, this value will be challenged by the private sector (where the user pays) and by value systems in the computing and telecommunications world (where charges for use of time and transactions is the norm). At this point in time, it is difficult to predict which will prevail.

" *The conflict between fee or tax funding for information services is not necessarily a dichotomy. In fact there will always be a mixed model that may change over time.* **"**

Kenneth E. Dowlin

From the point of view of managers making decisions today about tomorrow's strategic directions, we can only say that there will be more access to a richer mix of information, and that more is better, but not necessarily cheaper.

◆ The down side

Buses operate on fixed schedules but, by using them, it takes longer to get places. If a car-pool is set up, questions have to be answered such as who drives, which car is used, how are costs to be distributed among the participants. Both buses and ride-sharing mean that individuals have to make some personal accommodations. For example, smoking may be a problem and schedules do not always dovetail with individual needs.

So it is with information services and systems that are operated jointly or cooperatively by two or more organizations. Individual members have to make compromises. Group schedules, procedures, and standards have to be followed. Local freedoms and decisions are sometimes pre-empted by group goals and objectives – serious objections for some.

Even the promise of speedy delivery and desk-top access will not quell old arguments against inter-institutional cooperation. Not all faculty, librarians, and administrators will accept cost savings as a convincing rationale when it comes to sharing *their* library resources. Protestors echo the following sentiments:

- the library is already under-funded and should have a larger budget before it undertakes any other projects;
- unless materials are available locally, browsing and bibliographic research will be impaired;
- if the library relies on resources elsewhere, it will fall farther behind in national rankings;
- materials obtained from other places take too long to arrive;
- decent research requires immediate and convenient access at the local level;
- money spent on cooperation would be put to better use if spent on local library acquisitions.

Similarly, there may be misgivings about making local information systems and resources accessible to outsiders. In the private sector, information centers have an added fear that competitors will know too much about research and development information directions if information is sought from, or contributed to, a shared database. In short, companies want proprietary information protected, and want to put new knowledge to work before the competition can do so. When profits are at stake, company information centers want to receive information, not share it. The major concern in the not-for-profit sector is that sharing resources might put too much of a drain on local resources.

The best way to overcome such negative concerns is to demonstrate, through successes, that inter-institutional cooperation works to *improve* access to information, that it does not detract from local library support, that it does not affect profit margins, and that it produces economies of scale.

In assessing the costs and benefits of inter-institutional co-operation, each member will have to determine what factors are critical for demonstrating success to its constituency. Some basic questions that decision-makers must answer about a new or ongoing cooperative venture are:

- Does it add value or improve local systems and services?
- Does it effect savings at the local level?
- Does it offer local cost avoidance?
- Does it deepen and/or broaden the kind and nature of the materials, resources, or information that are accessible to local users?
- Does it break/eliminate barriers to information?
- Is it easy and relatively effort-free to manage and govern?
- Do local needs and priorities fit – or at least not conflict – with group values and goals?
- Do members control the venture?
- Does it provide more clout through collective action than was available to individual participants?
- Does it contribute to profit margins as well as sole source information services?

There are no decision packages that will determine the potential costs and benefits of inter-institutional cooperation. Behavioral issues such as territorial protectionism, fear of loss of autonomy, apprehensions about 'giving away the shop', and contributing 'more than our share' do not fit readily into a decision-making matrix. These, plus resistance from users who want it all in their own library, are the real issues that must be addressed. Visionary administrators who foresee the long-term benefits deriving from inter-institutional cooperation are in the best position to ensure success if cooperative information systems are the venue through which to provide more for less, or with the same amount of money.

Finally, many members fear that they will contribute more to a consortium than they get in return. To overcome some of these concerns, the information networks have tried to devise formulas that take into account the value that member libraries add to their databases. These efforts have not been totally successful, and now that local library systems are more sophisticated and can be interconnected, serious doubts are being raised about the continued viability of using shared databases for activities such as cataloging. These critics point out that they contribute piece-work at sweat-shop prices that the consortia then turn around and resell at a tidy profit (Lowry, 1990, p. 15). Defendants of cooperatives would argue that their pricing structures do try to compensate members who are net contributors. The perception of inequity, however, is difficult to dispel without hard data, and this, as discussed earlier in this chapter, is nearly non-existent.

In sum, while joint or shared routes to providing information services and resources hold much promise, they remain to be fully realized. The information technologies need to pass through several more generations development. More importantly, social, economic, and political infrastructures need to be developed to ensure that there is at least a modicum of standardization and organization in place to assuage the policy chaos that now exists.

The following two comments lend both an historical perspective and an insider's view to the discussion on the viability of cooperation. First, Robert M. Hayes:

" Throughout most of the long history of librarianship, its two imperatives – preservation of the records of the past and access to those records and their contents – have been mutually supportive. Libraries acquire materials, and access in the main was to be the resulting holdings of each particular library by the constituency it served; interlibrary loan was a valuable support, but its role was relatively limited and of minor significance in the overall. In this context, the concept of 'free' access was both meaningful and justifiable. The library, having made the capital investment in its collection, could easily make it freely available at essentially no additional cost, aside from wear and tear on the collection and the effects of use on availability. As a result, the library could serve its constituency within its budget and without the need to be concerned about the costs involved in meeting the needs for access. Even the real costs involved in interlibrary loan could be tolerated, given the relatively low level of use, the fiction of reciprocity, and the ability of the established staff to handle the workload.

Since the late thirties, though, increasingly the argument has been made that no library can stand alone and that inter-institutional cooperation, as a basis for 'sharing of resources', should be made a professional priority. At least one of the reasons was most clearly defined by Fremont Rider

– the exponential increase in collections and the resulting pressure to build ever more library buildings. After World War II, the problems were perceived to be even broader, as each major library faced increasing acquisitions of foreign materials, with the need not only to store them but to process them. The immediate result was the creation of cooperative activities; the Center for Research Libraries and the Farmington Plan were specific examples the former intended to deal with the problem of space and the latter with the acquisition of foreign materials.

For at least the last 30 years, these kinds of effort have steadily accelerated. The result has been an increased emphasis on sharing, aiming at replacing 'acquisition' with 'access' (meaning not just access to the individual collection, which was the historic emphasis, but access to materials wherever stored, especially elsewhere). Some efforts have resulted in mechanisms to facilitate inter-institutional cooperation with sharing of resources as a major objective, creating networks and other organizational structures to coordinate the efforts with these objectives in mind. Some have aimed at developing centralized facilities (some ideas based on expanding the Center for Research Libraries, others on replicating the highly successful Lending Division of the British Library) as a means to supplement if not replace local acquisition. Some were fostered by federal funding explicitly directed at encouraging the development of 'multi-type' networks at the state level, with resource-sharing as the watchword. Some created bibliographic utilities, intended in part to facilitate the process of interlibrary lending.

Today, the emphasis on 'access' has reached a near-crescendo, as the voices of the purveyors of electronic forms of information access and some university administrators add to those of librarians. The enthusiasts present the vision of electronic information as the wave of the future, and at least some administrators see that vision as the solution to the 'library problem', as a means to avoid building new libraries to house what they see as ever-increasing collections. The potential represented by the National Research and Education Network is seen as replacing books and journals with real 'information', instantly available, current, and readily processed.

*What a vision and what a combination of incentives!
'Access' means we will not need to spend money on books,
journals, buildings, and staff! 'Access' means that we will
have instant information, with all of the technology of
computer processing for retrieval, analysis, and presentation!
'Access' means that scholars will be able to communicate
directly with 'information' as well as with each other, without
the need to go to a library and face the problem of finding
there what they want! 'Access' means speed and efficiency
and currency!*

Of course, the reality is that libraries are still vitally
important and the gap between electronic potentials and
current reality is still so great that librarians must continue to
focus their attention on the proper balance today between the
benefits and costs of acquisition and access, including those
associated with inter-institutional cooperation. The benefits
have in part been alluded to already: cooperation implies
better utilization of the money spent for acquisitions by
reduction in unnecessary duplication among libraries. By
sharing resources, by treating the major libraries of the
country virtually as a single collection, each library and the
constituency it serves has access to more materials than
would otherwise be the case. Growth in holdings at individual
libraries can occur at a slower pace, so there is lessened need
for construction of new library buildings.

The costs of access, of sharing, of inter-institutional
cooperation, though, are not usually discussed by the
enthusiasts. It is almost as if the perception is that the benefits
all come free. The reality, of course, is that there are very real
costs associated with access. Even in earlier, simpler times,
when access meant interlibrary loan and use was relatively
limited, the major net lenders – especially the prestigious
private universities – found the costs and effects on their own
constituencies to be burdensome. They argued repeatedly and
still do today, that there should be some mechanism for
reimbursement, at least of the direct costs incurred.

In that respect, it is relevant to note that libraries generally
have under-estimated the costs for these kind of activities.
They will frequently consider only the direct costs, ignoring
even the most evident of overhead costs (such as salary
related benefits and costs of supervision); that in itself results

in estimates that are half of the true costs. The result is that comparisons of access and alternatives and of benefits with costs are biased.

In fact, the studies that have been made of ILL costs suggest totals, for both borrowing and lending libraries together, on the order of $30.00 per transaction. And commercial 'document delivery services' as replacements for the lending library will be charging fees that will result in roughly comparable total costs. Given those costs specifically associated with access, even a relatively low rate of use easily justifies acquisition instead of access. Indeed, an analysis of benefits versus costs is likely to demonstrate that current acquisition policies of major university libraries are close to optimum.

But beyond the costs directly attributable to access are those associated with the mechanisms of cooperation. Memberships in consortia carry their own costs – indirect as well as direct. Indeed, in many respects, the commitment of upper levels of library management to the management of cooperative arrangements represent exceptionally high expenditures of resources. These 'general and administrative' costs need to be recognized as decisions are made about access allocations. Furthermore, as increasing numbers of libraries install automated 'local systems', each must make decisions concerning input to the national databases in order to maintain those means so needed to facilitate inter-institutional sharing of resources. Again, costs will be incurred, obviously necessary but also part of the balance in the assessment of benefits versus costs. **"**

Robert M. Hayes

And from K. Wayne Smith:

" What price cooperation? That is the fundamental question which underlies the authors' discussion in this chapter on cooperative routes. The authors describe the changing nature of cooperation among institutions and professionals and the ongoing debate about the potential costs and benefits of such cooperation.

Historically, libraries have cooperated for both tangible and intangible reasons. There are three main tangible reasons: to save money; to improve services; and to assist with the functions of organizing, storing, preserving, and providing access to information. The primary intangible reason is to increase and advance knowledge. While the means to cooperate vary with the technologies that have been available at particular points in time, the ends of cooperation tend not to vary.

Take, for example, the science journal. The first science journal, Philosophical Transactions, began publication in 1655 'to search, try and find out new things, impart their knowledge to one another, and contribute what they can to the Grand Design of improving Natural knowledge . . .' (Boorstin, 1983). In 1992, OCLC and the American Association for the Advancement of Science will introduce the world's first, peer-reviewed electronic science journal in order to respond to the pressing need for faster access to new medical research. Clearly, the more the means to cooperate change, the more the ends of cooperation remain the same. Nearly 500 years later, people still cooperate and share information with an eye toward the Grand Design.

The price of cooperation, though, fluctuates in a complex information marketplace that involves public and private sectors operating on local, regional, national and, increasingly, international levels.

The OCLC computer library network is a case in point. OCLC began in 1971 as a regional library network serving 54 libraries in the state of Ohio. It was founded by college and university presidents who believed that their institutions could reduce the rate of rise of library costs and increase the availability of library resources through an online shared cataloging system that would create an online union catalog of the holdings of Ohio's academic libraries.

It is fair to say that the growth of the OCLC network from an intra-state one, to an international network linking over 13 500 libraries in 46 countries in 1991 has been one of the success stories of inter-institutional cooperation. Through cooperation, libraries have built the OCLC Online Union Catalog into the world's premier bibliographic database. It contains more than 25 million records and grows at a rate of about two million records annually. This cooperative, computerized catalog provides the bibliographic information needed to drive a host of internal library operations. It has saved libraries a lot of time and money.

The cooperation that built the OCLC database has also placed new worlds of information at the fingertips of scholars, researchers, and students. For example, a library user connected to the OCLC database, irrespective of his or her geographical location, can now efficiently and effectively navigate through a catalog that represents a significant portion of the world's knowledge – a merged catalog of 13 500 libraries. They can then use the OCLC Interlibrary Loan Subsystem to arrange to have the materials sent to their location. In 1991, for example, libraries conducted more than 5.4 million interlibrary loans in this fashion.

Clearly, for the first 20 years of OCLC's online existence, the price has been right for cooperation via centralized computer networks. Indeed, by the mid-1990s OCLC will have provided its member libraries with more than $1 billion in products and services – based on cooperative cataloging and resource sharing.

Yet, the world has changed since OCLC introduced its shared cataloging system. Then, large central computer systems and their economies of scale made economic sense and practical sense. Now, distributed processing, powerful microcomputers and other technological advances have changed some of the basic assumptions. The Internet, the NREN, and other local, regional, national and international networks hold out the promise of 'free' telecommunications services. Local library systems reduce the need for collaboration and timely sharing of resources and information. Some libraries now find it more cost-effective to do their own cataloging on local systems and consult the OCLC database only if they are unable to find information in their own systems. Also, local and regional networks are now able to take advantage of advances in technology to establish local and regional resource sharing networks that use OCLC only when they cannot find what they need locally or regionally.

At the same time, library users themselves have become increasingly sophisticated and have greatly increased expectations about the level of service their libraries provide, irrespective of their geographic location or their libraries' local holdings. The plot is further thickened by the sheer growth of the information and knowledge base. Libraries face an information Armageddon. The pressures in academia to publish are unrelenting. Specialization knows no bounds. Thus, the number of journal titles, reports and monographs continues to spiral upward annually, exceeded only by their spiralling costs. The number of electronic databases is steadily increasing. Efficient navigation of this vast ocean of information will require more cooperation among libraries than ever before.

In the future, libraries will have to continue to cooperate to meet the needs and expectations of their users. Resource sharing is inherently cooperative. The advancement of knowledge depends on cooperation and the sharing of information routinely and efficiently.

OCLC has been built on cooperation and resource sharing and achieving the lowest possible cost. It has also been built with the idea of harnessing cooperation to provide information to people when and where they need it, in a form they want, at a price they can afford. Providing bibliographic information has been a giant first step toward providing other kinds of information – abstracts, indexes and, eventually, the full text of documents, journal articles and monographs. Indeed, it is a natural extension for OCLC to move from indexes and bibliography to primary sources of information, such as the online electronic journal mentioned earlier.

In the future, library cooperation will be increasingly electronic, but it will continue to serve traditional purposes. Those cooperative electronic endeavors that avoid duplication of effort, that generate economies of scale, that reduce costs, and that increase access to information must also be economically viable. While most of us would agree that the price of cooperation ought to be determined by something more than a crass economic calculus, we would also agree that the question of how best to serve the public good, frequently boils down to economics. Put another way, the price of electronic cooperation seems likely to remain what we are willing to pay. **"**

K. Wayne Smith

7 Costs and charging strategies

- ◆ Dysfunctions in traditional systems
- ◆ Cost recovery
- ◆ Computing and networking costs
- ◆ Pricing information
- ◆ Full cost-recovery model

The fiscal environment for information services organizations rarely changes dramatically – even if parent organizations cut financial resources dramatically. Similarly, traditional sources of funding and library reliance on external 'beneficence' seldom alter. There are omens, however, that this relatively stable milieu is collapsing. This chapter explores the changes that are causing information services to reassess their traditional views of funding sources, and the costs and charge-backs for their operations. Among the major factors contributing to the need for radical change in fiscal attitudes is the basic market shift from selling to 'leasing' by information suppliers. Another is the pressure for information service centers to generate more of their own funds and rely less and less on 'central' beneficence. In short, there is pressure to accommodate both outsourcing (as opposed to owner-ship) and cost recovery (not 'free' service) for information.

As many information service organizations move to service policies that are based on access in lieu of ownership, one of the critical questions that must be faced is what is the most economical and effective way to provide information in a given situation. In terms of the search for specific information for example, is an online search of an external database more economical than an on-site manual search? Or, should the external database be leased for on-site use through a CD-ROM file server in order to create economies of scale? If the automated search process proves more economical than manual methods, should the inferior paper product be canceled in favor of accessing information through electronic means? If the information requested is in a little-used journal, should that subscription be canceled in favor of facsimile services through a document delivery supplier?

This chapter will address the question of what is entailed in an information service center moving toward a more appropriate financial response to the external trends mentioned above. A model is presented for analysis and allocation of costs that can guide decision-makers in shifting from traditional budgeting schemes toward cost-recovery systems.

66 *The issues delineated in this chapter are problems for most libraries and information centers. Corporate information centers like other information providers, are undergoing radical changes: in types of services provided; in the technologies used to deliver information; and in the traditional and computerized methods of delivery services. Costs have not shifted from printed books and journals to the information technologies. In order to hold costs at a steady state, some information centers now maintain only a small book collection. They have also eliminated less frequently used journals if the full text is available online. While these measures can increase cost-effectiveness, there remains a constant need for justification for continuing the existence of the corporate information center. The defense of the library is now coupled with a growing requirement that it recover all costs for services.* 99

Elsie Stephens

◆ Dysfunctions in traditional systems

Information service centers have moved from labor-intensive and manual operations to functioning in a distributed and collaborative mode in both organizing and providing access to information. Increased use of information technologies are highlighting the fact that traditional budget cycles and funding sources are inadequate for handling a volatile technological infrastructure. Similarly, the information marketplace is nudging a redefinition of the traditional role of information service organizations as being 'just-in-case' consumers to being 'just-in-time providers'. As a result, the budgeting and cost allocation processes that were appropriate in the past are being taxed to remain responsive. Different approaches are needed that are more apt. A strong contender is a philosophical shift toward cost recovery.

Although the operating environment of most information service organizations can be described as dynamic and in a constant state of planned and reactionary change, most, in fact, operate from year to year under a conventional line item budget. They either have budget lines for each type of expense, or operate under some form of a program budget where line items are allocated to different functions performed within the organization, e.g. information retrieval. On some settings there is a painfully clear demarkation between funds allocated for books and funds that can be used for other goods and services. It is not uncommon, for example, for funding agencies to insist on policies, particularly in tough times, that reduce all parts of a library budget except for the portion allocated for 'books'. In some government circles, this distinction is drawn so finely that databases (online or on CD-ROMs) cannot be charged against the 'book budget'.

“ *Cost allocation is certainly becoming more important as managers try to handle the leasing or ownership problem, but many managers see the costs associated with the new technologies as a normal part of the materials budget, allocated just as other subscriptions are handled. The 'pressure' to generate funds is usually an internal decision caused by overall budget restrictions. Those who feel strongly about not charging fees, deny that format makes any difference at all in materials allocations.* **”**

Robert Croneberger

Normally the budget process in most information service operations is based on a cost-allocation method, sometimes augmented by cost recovery. In some, but relatively few instances, a total cost-recovery method is used. Cost allocation attempts to identify the proportion of the organization's costs that are appropriately attributed to either specific users of, or departments that provide, information services. If the costs are not attributed to the users in this cost-appointment process, they are sometimes attributed to specific inputs or outputs of the organization, such as number of books acquired or number of database searches performed. Regardless of whether or not the organization is operated on some kind of cost-recovery basis, the process of cost allocation has been used by most organizations at least in a macro or gross way to provide an information service center with an annual budget.

In general, there is not a strong tradition to use sound managerial accounting practices in information services. They have tended to justify financial need less on analysis of costs than on defense of historically allocated funds and arguments for incremental increases. Because we believe that information service centers will be faced with the need to recover more and more of their costs, the next section explores how cost recovery has traditionally been used by this sector. A later section then outlines a model for developing full cost-recovery information services.

" *In many corporate settings, funds are appropriated to libraries by historical allotment and use of benefit analysis to argue for additional products and services. Cost of the library and its direct and indirect costs are usually billed back to departments based upon internal corporate accounting practices. Corporate beneficence is fading. In many organizations, research and other information services are outsourced to information brokers and database producers. Outsourcing reduces the indirect costs of space, utilities, and maintenance. Many corporate information centers are being placed in a competitive position with outsourcing firms and are increasingly asked to recover their total operating costs. The hurdle for information center managers is thus to develop a sound pricing policy for any or all of its costs.* "*

Elsie Stephens

◆ Cost recovery

Cost recovery has been used in some situations to transfer the cost (or some part of the cost) of running the information service organization to users or departments/agencies served either through direct charges or some form of budget subvention. This is a more common practice in the corporate community. It is less often used in other settings and, as mentioned earlier in this book, clashes with some of the traditional value systems held by information professionals.

135

Cost finding as an analytical tool on which to base cost recovery schemes has a relatively short history of use in information services. Cost finding is a form of cost analysis which, if done well, will justify the budget of the information service, measure program efficiency, allow cost comparisons of various cost-recovery schemes, and inform management and users of the cost of key services.

66 Knowing the cost of any service does not justify that service. What is the societal value of circulating mysteries? We cannot assume that cost-allocation models justify anything. When telefacsimile technology was first introduced, automobile companies in Detroit concluded that they did not need information that fast, and refused to pay for the equipment needed to fax materials. Maybe decisions like that are an indication of the state of the industry today. 99

Robert Croneberger

If an organization is funded according to some sort of cost-recovery scheme, the following types of services are examples of what can be charged back to users: manual reference searches, online reference searches, interlibrary loan, document delivery, photocopying, current awareness services, consulting services, indexing services, translation services, and customized bibliography services.

If these cost-recovery services are to primary clientele of the organization, charge-back policies can be based on a variety of principles:

1. Direct costs plus overhead or indirect costs – when indirect and/or overhead costs are included in cost-recovery calculations, most information centers tend to be less than comprehensive in their inclusions;
2. Direct costs only – this is most often used as the basis of cost-recovery since they are the easiest to identify;
3. A flat fee – in settings where equality of access is an issue, such as public libraries, a flat (and usually minimal) fee is often the basis for recovering a portion of the costs for operating a service;
4. A sliding scale of fees has been used in some settings where it is assumed that some have less ability to pay full costs (e.g. students) than others (e.g. faculty);
5. A subsidized rate – like the sliding scale, this is usually used in

situations when it is known that users cannot afford to pay full costs.

Often when services are provided to non-primary clientele (third parties, e.g. businesses, industry, etc., in the case of a college or university) charges for information services are configured differently, and differentially.

❝ There is no 'non-primary' clientele, and since businesses and corporations pay taxes on their businesses, they are entitled to information from the public library. ❞

Robert Croneberger

They may, for example, include a standard fee plus a surcharge on direct costs incurred for services like a database search. Other constructs could mean application of a standard fee plus a flat rate surcharge or a standard fee with a multiplier surcharge. Another approach used is to set up a contractual arrangement that provides for a certain level of service for either an annual fee or a subscription fee. The kinds of services offered might be similar to those provided by information brokers (see Chapter 3), and typically include document delivery, online searching or research, verification of facts or citations, translation, compilation of data or information, and preparation of digests or reports. As a source of income for information centers, relatively few public and academic libraries have succeeded in recovery of their total costs for these types of services to their non-primary clientele. One of the factors contributing to this phenomenon is that information service providers have a hard time putting a price on their 'goods and services'.

Prices are used in society to allocate goods and services, to differentiate between alternate goods and services, and to provide incentives for individuals to choose between alternative goods and services. The prices set by information service organizations for their services (whether for full or partial cost recovery) do not necessarily bear a relationship to value, nor do they even represent an appropriate return on the cost of providing a particular information service. Ideally, the value of information services should be set and measured on the basis of the organization's performance or actual output in terms of productivity, efficiency, and effectiveness in providing goods or a particular service. In turn, those goods or services must be valued from the perspective of their effect on the user's work (time and effort), and the effect of the user's work on society, e.g. increased productivity, increased capacity to compete, improved quality of life, etc.

Before the value and price for information services can be decided, there are some policy questions to be answered. Is the organization setting fees to ration services that were not budgeted or were underbudgeted? Is equity of service a concern if fees are set, or will services be provided on the basis of ability to pay? Will the administrative costs of collecting fees be greater than the fees collected? Based on the ultimate value of the service to society, are the fees apportioned in recognition of that value?

> " There must be a fundamental change in thrust and vision from ownership of materials to access to information. Many corporations have either PC- or mainframe-based information systems that support mounting of external databases or the dissemination of information throughout the corporation. Use of these technologies will require librarians to rethink the acquisition of books and journals at traditional spending levels in order to create the opportunity to reduce space and the accompanying costs. This change in practise would allow information centers to develop prices that are competitive with external information providers. "

> *Elsie Stephens*

De Gennaro (1989) says that 'we have seen the relative stability of the 1960s give way to the volatile changes of the 1970s and 1980s. We are experiencing a number of historic swings in our society. Government ownership is out, privatization is in; government controls are out, business and free enterprise are in; welfare is out, self-reliance is in; centralization is out, localization is in; free is out, fee is in'. He also states the greatest challenge in the next decade is to implement new entrepreneurial management structures and cultures 'in our ailing industrial-age libraries'. This does not imply the need to abandon the perspective of information as a free good, but rather to adopt the perspective that information services are becoming increasingly dependent upon commercial suppliers, as well as becoming commercial information suppliers themselves.

In tough economic times, there will be a strong temptation for information professionals to assume a for-profit orientation. This urge will require a rethinking of old values, unprecedented search for innovation, the creation of new services and new uses of traditional budgets. It will also test the values and precepts that have safeguarded equal and free access to information.

" The argument that allows libraries to charge patrons for use of electronic databases is specious, at best. It amounts to a discrimination by format which public libraries have always rejected in the past.

We do not charge patrons for their use of one volume of an encyclopedia, nor for a single journal in a subscription. Nor should we be charging fees for access to a portion of an electronic database. "

Robert Croneberger

When new electronic resources were first introduced, it seemed as though organizations that did not provide access to them were providing inferior service. It also appeared as though changes were so rapid and dynamic that information centers were being outstripped in their ability to pay for them without add-on charges to recover some of these costs. With time, budgets have been altered somewhat to accommodate these new information formats. It has also helped somewhat that the publishers of these products provide them through leases or as subscriptions. This has allowed for more flexibility in budgeting for them and has reduced the need for rationing through cost-recovery schemes.

The real challenge is for information professionals to rethink the use of their acquisitions budgets as more and more material appear only in electronic formats. In 1982 it was estimated (Lancaster, 1982) that by the year 2000, 50 per cent of all indexes and abstracts would be available only in electronic format. The shift may in fact be slower than anticipated a decade ago but acquisitions budgets in this environment must, of necessity, shift and become viewed as access budgets. Within this context, cost allocation, not necessarily cost recovery, becomes the information service management issue of the decade. One of the critical components of cost analyses in this environment will be the computing and networking costs associated with housing and serving up access to information that exists only in electronic form.

" The costs of online searches must be part of the acquisitions budget of each department using electronic search tools. The

decision to use an electronic search must be made by the staff, not by the user. Use of a database would not be different than use of any of the other tools that a library has at its command.

Non-ownership of information is not a justification for the imposition of fees. A library does not 'own' a journal to which it subscribes and houses for public use. The same is true for electronic databases. The decision to cancel hard copy is a management one, triggered by the cost of space, retrieval time, and search capability. The saving accrued by the decision not to have hard copy of a journal must be used to access that journal by electronic means, without passing the costs on to the user.

A more apt comparison would be to begin charging for the costs of storing hard copies of journals, retrieval time, and manual search time. Just as this would be absurd, it is absurd to charge users for the costs of accessing electronic databases. **"**

Robert Croneberger

◆ Computing and networking costs

As with the information containers themselves, organizations have the option of operating the requisite computing and network systems in-house, leasing them, or outsourcing them. In larger information service centers it is not uncommon to operate stand-alone systems for at least bibliographic information and databases. More commonly, information centers rely on computing facilities elsewhere in the organization for computing and data network services. In the context of this book it is important for the latter arrangement to be understood.

For information service organizations that do not operate their own computing facility, a significant part of their budget could be expended on a contract arrangement with a computing center either within or outside the parent institution (see Chapter 5 for a discussion of outsourcing and purchase of hardware and software for library systems). If a cost-recovery contract is drawn up with a computing center, it is important to understand the changes in their environment. In the past 20 years the role of centralized computing services has changed dramatically. New services are being provided in response to new technology, and some traditional services are being discontinued or distributed. The most obvious change is that computing users are no longer totally dependent on mainframe computing because many functions can be accomplished at the desk-top level. Likewise, central support of applications programming is no longer the norm, and new programming languages and applications packages require specialized knowledge, again diminishing the central role of the computing center to apply them. This is particularly true at the information service center level.

Alterations in centralized computing services, then, are the direct result of increased use of microcomputers and added responsibility for telecommunications. While older services might have been viewed as institutional overhead, new services such as networks are often budgeted on a cost-recovery basis. One of the most obvious new centralized computing services is networking. Distributed computing requires that individual machines be linked in order to share access, data, printers, software, etc. For information service centers, not only is local network access to software, data files, file servers, and peripheral hardware an issue, but so is connection to international, national, regional and other local computing and network services. In this kind of environment, information service centers will need help with software acquisitions, negotiating and operating institution-wide site licenses, and support to provide on-site fixes for software and hardware dedicated to information dissemination.

Computing centers have also begun to provide information and communication services, providing database access, institution-wide electronic mail, bulletin boards, directories, tele-conferencing, and instruction and consulting advice to users. Information service centers can end up being both partners and consumers of centralized or external suppliers of computing and telecommunications systems, in order to operate and maintain their own information system. In this context, the information center can assume that some sort of cost recovery scheme will be in place, imposing charges for things such as the following:

1. Support for operations services, including general administrat-

ive and facility operating expenses, and technical staff support for systems and networking;

2. The installation, license and annual charges for the vendor's system software;
3. Local site preparation;
4. Central site hardware and software (including telecommunications and operating system enhancements) needed for the information system's installation and maintenance; and
5. Travel reimbursement for computer center staff to attend technical seminars, workshops, etc. related to the operation of the information system.

With respect to networking, many institutions consider the cost of telecommunications support for local networks to be an institutional overhead. Others levy a monthly service or equipment fee to participating units. The cost to move beyond the local network and link to external networks such as the Internet or EARN is likewise often borne by the parent institution. At present, the cost of the Internet is shared by participating agencies and various levels of government, and is only vaguely felt or appreciated by individuals at the local level.

In future, however, information centers can anticipate chargebacks based on use of and demand for network capacity. According to Roberts (1990), 'any unit of measure we adopt for network charging has to meet the criteria of having a clear relationship to the average user's perception of value in using the network, and it must be able to prospectively affect user behavior in the direction of more effective and efficient use of the network'. Budget planners for information service organizations should therefore be aware that their access budgets will probably be affected by additional value-added charges for network use.

Just as computing and networking are requiring unprecedented elasticity in information service center budgets, so are the information 'goods' themselves.

◆ Pricing information

Producers and publishers of information are experiencing the same radical shift from manual to electronic operations as everyone else. The capital developmental and research costs needed to shift to computer-based operations and output is straining traditional marketing and pricing systems. The changing economics of the information chain, particularly the part grounded in scholarly, scientific and technical communication in the academic community, have been widely discussed in the literature. These cases are perhaps an accurate microcosm of the issues facing all information service organizations and the publications they acquire. Okerson and Stubbs (1991) found, for example, that between 1985–86 to 1989–90, prices of monographs for academic libraries rose 41 per cent, resulting in a 16 per cent drop in actual monographs purchased, or about 570 000 fewer monographs on the shelves of these libraries. Likewise, as mentioned earlier, these same libraries paid 52 per cent more for journal subscriptions, but held 1 per cent fewer subscriptions. Subscriptions are obviously being maintained at the expense of monograph purchases.

The factors driving this economic shift are many and varied. Aside from the common explanations which include the increased costs of production and distribution, factors such as dramatic fluctuations in currencies worldwide also have an impact. Petersen (1990) has also documented that publisher type, country of origin, and the subject discipline are non-cost factors that also influence journal prices. To these must also be added some institutional factors from the academic community. These include quantitative vs. qualitative standards of excellence, the steady increase in the cost of higher education and research, reduced subsidization of research, and the rising costs associated with maintaining and retaining authors. These institutional factors (which include in some quarters the reassertion of intellectual property rights and the expectation that faculty will generate consumable information), if aggressively pursued, could conceivably result in a redefinition of standards of excellence in higher education. They could also mean there will be efforts to do one or all of the following: capitalize the world's intellectual output; privatize intellectual property; develop a communications process dominated by marketplace policies; increase the cost of publications; and, perhaps, stem the free exchange of information.

" Privatization of government information has led to a
   declining value of the databases being produced in two ways.
   First, since the information being disseminated goes to the
   lowest bidder, commercial firms are hiring lower paid staff to

produce databases. As a result, they are becoming more difficult to use. "

Robert Croneberger

The ideal basis for pricing publications would be access to a wide diversity of publications as a matter of public policy and social investment. This would require a wide array of publication outlets that generate reasonably priced, high-quality information. If this were in place, one or more of the necessary prerequisites to successful discriminatory pricing of publications could be eliminated according to Talaga and Haley (1991). In this ideal world, the type of value-added processes in document-based systems described by Taylor (1984) would drive the utility, as well as the value and price of publications.

Until such a paragon of pricing is achieved, the most equitable way to establish journal prices would appear to be use of a price-per-words method. Meyers (1991) found that while this method did not account for differences in quality, it can be viewed as a reasonably equitable quantitative tool. This, coupled with deliberations on quality between information professionals and authors should suffice as an effective means to eliminate low quality, highly priced journals. In turn this could lead to the kind of scenario wherein journal publishers would negotiate pricing packages with information service organizations or groups of them, based on purchasing levels.

Book dealers engage in these types of negotiations as a part of their standard operating business practices. Another place to start such negotiations would be on discount rates based on the elimination of postage charges. In other words, as publishers go through the process of upgrading their business systems, as they must, the resultant improvements in operations should see some restructuring to include more quantification of pricing processes in relation to clients' goals and standards. This would mean a radical differentiation of purchasing services in order to be responsive to the different requirements of different organizations or groups of organizations. The primary focus would be to price information so that publishers' offerings support distinctive organizational characteristics and purchasing levels.

While the search continues for more viable pricing strategies, the traditional print milieu pricing strategies remain in flux and under stress for both technological and economic reasons. Another area where pricing policies of information suppliers and producers is causing great confusion is in the use of electronic products in a network environment.

Publishers of CD-ROM products typically charge a hefty fee for basic lease of their products and then add surcharges for network access. The base prices are often set on various grounds such as type of library, and/or size of user population and can range from a thousand dollars to $30 000.[1] The surcharges for network access can present a confusing picture for managers who are trying to determine whether to lease such products for in-house use or to outsource their information services. Similarly, with differential charging by CD-ROM publishers, information centers can themselves be caught in a maze that obscures their cost analyses.

In 1991, for example, The H.W. Wilson Company added a 50 per cent surcharge for their networked CD-ROM products to corporate libraries for each additional site or office with remote access plus a ten per cent charge for each potential simultaneous remote user. College and university libraries were charged ten per cent of the annual subscription rate for each potential simultaneous remote user as were public libraries. The latter, however, were also charged ten per cent per branch for remote access. Other vendors have different charging algorithms. While not impossible, it is increasingly difficult for decision-makers to determine which information service configuration is most cost-effective with such diverse and changing pricing structures. The simplest may just be to buy all information service needs at set costs from brokers or fee-based enterprises within traditional libraries. If this is done, at least the burden of establishing prices for services is shifted to another party.

" Database producers and leasers of information must develop better and more standardized pricing structures for the new information formats such as abstracts and full text on magnetic tape and compact disk, since they are generally made accessible by information centers on the corporate network. Database producers often develop pricing structures

---

[1] In 1991, *SciSearch* annual costs were $30 000.00, and *Psychological Abstracts* on tape charged an annual lease fee of $7 500.00 for a current subscription plus an annual license fee of $1 500.00. The H.W. Wilson Company charged according to a formula that took into account the size of the user population plus the cost of its paper indexes.

for electronic products in the same way as print products. The present per terminal price structure is unworkable when large numbers of employees have networked PCs or terminals on their desks. Users end up paying overly high costs on this basis. Since there is a marginal increase in value per terminal connected, the vendor's pricing structure should be altered to reflect these economies of scale. **"**

Elsie Stephens

With the advent of technologies like CD-ROM, and the growing availability of lease arrangements with database producers through which tapes can be mounted locally on a subscription basis, the volume of online searching of remote databases is decreasing in many information centers. At present, charging schemes for these services include the user paying the direct costs of the connect time to the vendor only, direct costs plus overhead, a flat fee, or on a sliding scale, or paying at a subsidized rate. In the end, connect-time charging is a disincentive that actually discourages the optimal use of remote databases. This is because connect-time pricing does not relate to the resources used or to the information retrieved. We believe that the future of online searching lies in non-mediated, self-searching. This implies a need for a totally new way to sell and price these remote-access products – where the user is able to budget for the search, determining before the search begins how much will be spent in order to obtain the information needed. For example, a combination of subscription and offline print costs or discount pricing may work here. The bottom line with online searching is that it has a distinct future, but only if the charge-back schemes of database vendors and information service organizations are changed to accommodate end-user searching, particularly in an environment that has faster and smarter hardware.

For individuals or information service centers that have to establish a price for their goods and services as brokers or disseminators, the prices they pay for information is making it increasingly difficult for them to be able to determine what full cost recovery means. Ironically, the trend toward outsourcing makes it imperative that both information brokers (be they individuals or traditional libraries) and their customers understand the basis for the prices that are charged and paid. For this reason, a framework must be available that enables construction of an understandable and workable formula to establish how an information service can recover the full costs of the goods and services it provides.

◆ Full cost-recovery model

" *Users of systems and services will pay full costs. Good communication, surveys and marketing tools must be used to ensure that information centers are providing products and services that users need. Similarly, there must be a constant evaluation of the products and services to ensure that corporate end-users are receiving useful information. If information products and services are deemed valuable by corporate users and prices are competitive, cost recovery is achievable.* **"**

Elsie Stephens

Before describing what a full cost-recovery model might be like, it must be emphasized that the information service professions have traditionally used fees to ration access to information. A prime example of this is the establishment by public and academic libraries of fee-based information services to third parties (e.g. people living outside a public library's designated service area, business and industry, economic development agencies, etc.). Granted, these services provide a valued community service, and establish closer economic, cultural, and professional development ties between the library and its immediate and corporate community. They also provide a lift to the income side of the ledger. Academic libraries, for example, reason that such differentially priced fee-based services are an extension of institutional fund-raising; they enrich collection development and library instruction capacities, and provide users with the advantage of having access to a greater variety of resources.

So there is precedent for fee-based services within the professional ethos of providing free access. The Library Association in the UK published guidelines on charging which recognize that 'it is not considered practicable for all conceivable library and information services to be provided by the public sector free of charge to all who demand them in all circumstances' (Norton, 1988).

147

Some libraries rationalize partial or full cost recovery on the basis of providing value-added services. The Los Angeles County Library, for example, charges a fee for mail delivery of audio cassettes even though they use the following slogan to market themselves: 'the best things in life are free'. They reason that 'people can still come into the library and get an audio free; we are only charging for mail service – a value-added service' (Los Angeles, 1991).

" *Charging fees undermines the mission of the public library. If we begin to charge fees for the use of material, all tax dollars in support of libraries should be discontinued. How many private citizens could then support the costs of renting a book, or a video tape, or getting information from a database? The public library systems in North America were based on the ideals of a democratic society. All citizens pay for access to the same information, whatever the format.*

Or perhaps we have concluded that democracy is too expensive a form of government?

The seriously deteriorating economic conditions of our local governments have given new impetus to the 'free vs. fee' issue in many libraries. The debate is most heated in public libraries but does occur in other settings.

There is a great deal of discussion about artificial distinctions in public service, sometimes called 'value-added' services. The argument appears to say that 'basic' services should remain free, but value-added services may require additional charges to be supported. Administrators, or course, are the ones who define which services are basic and which are value-added.

I would argue that a library is, by definition, a value-added service and always has been. A room full of books is not a library. Arrange them in some order, catalog them, classify them, create a card catalog so they might be found on the shelves, and you have begun a value-added service. Answer questions from these books for people who need help, maybe even over the telephone, telefax pages from them, send needed titles to other libraries – all these are value-added services that enhance that original 'room full of books'. Tell stories from them to children and adults, take an autoharp and guitar and sing songs from some of them, entice people to read and use them in any way possible — these are the value-added services that constitute a library.

These value-added services have always been free to the public in North America because they are already paid for by the people who use them. They are supported by public taxes.

The mission of the public library has been to use these tax dollars to provide these value-added services. There is absolutely no justification for any additional charges.

Video tapes are a good example. Renting video tapes is foreign to the mission of public libraries, no matter how much money can be collected. The same has been true for best sellers. Some libraries charge a small amount for the postcard that informs users that their reserved item is now available. But the costs of maintaining this procedure are never fully recovered. Some believe that the imposition of a small fee will reduce the number of reserves called for, but that is not borne out in many studies. Even so, it is clearly a management problem, not a fiscal one. **"**

Robert Croneberger

There are, of course, more than economic considerations involved in deciding whether or not to establish a fee-based service for non-primary clientele. Philosophical issues as well as ease of collecting cost information are the primary ones. In traditional library settings, most fee-based services are for express document delivery, online database searches, custom research, specialized training and consultation, translations, verification, book reserves, etc. Charges for these services are usually based on one or more of the following patterns:

1. **A token fee** – a nominal charge that prevents abuse while not deterring use of a service, such as the cost of mailing a post card for the privilege of reserving a best seller.
2. **A uniform fee** – a charge that is established for each service on the basis of the actual unit cost of the service such as $10.00 for verifying a citation and $25.00 for an online literature search of up to 20 citations.
3. **Standardized fee** – like a uniform charge, but a fee agreed upon by all information centers irrespective of their actual or local costs.
4. **Variable or incremental fees** – charges levied on the basis of

each transaction but varying with the volume or production of services provided, or with the costs incurred when an additional 'unit' of service is provided. While the most rational, this method of cost analysis is difficult and time-consuming to apply in information service settings.

5. **Total cost recovery** – the fees charged to users would reflect the full cost of providing the service. Some might even add a 'profit' margin to realize real income.

The last option is one that sits least well with traditional library operations. For example, the Council of Federal Libraries in Canada (Council of Federal Libraries, 1981) decided that passing total charges onto users is a feasible option in their environment, but argued that it is extremely difficult to calculate the costs because of the intangible costs of government. As more and more information centers are confronted by technological and economic turbulence, they will be challenged to operate under conditions that require near or full cost recovery. The corporate community somehow manages to operate service industries and calculate both costs and profit margins. The companies to which entire agencies, including libraries, are outsourced by governments in their efforts to privatize, are somehow able to determine what to bid and how to maintain a competitive edge in 'soft' and 'intangible' service sectors. Surely if information brokers can determine fees that reflect the full cost plus a profit, so can traditional information workers that operate within the environs of a library or information center.

Whether it is from the point of view of negotiating with a broker (as a seller or buyer of information) or from the point of view of leasing out (of or for) information services, the costs that are contracted for become negotiable yet have a predictable set of elements. The basis for payment (annual fee, pay-as-you-go) is at once independent of the cost elements and negotiable. Most difficulty in determining full cost recovery then lies in defining the elements that are to be included. They must of necessity include both direct and indirect costs. The list below is a mix of both, since direct costs in one service can become the indirect costs in another.

The following checklist can be used by an information center that wants to determine how to establish a fee-based service to recover full costs. On a number of the elements, the center may have to confront and clarify value systems, policies, and politics.

From the perspective of the manager seeking to outsource information services, the list is a guide for negotiating the price.

1. Personnel – salaries and benefits;
2. Equipment purchased specifically for the service, as well as that purchased for support functions – including amortization, maintenance contracts and repair costs;
3. Office space – utilities, janitorial costs, wear and tear on equipment and furnishings such as chairs and carpets;
4. Proportionate costs of the historical collections and collections space – in other words, what is the value of the portion of the collections used by the service;
5. Use of the collections – circulation, wear and tear, preservation, binding, and proportionate costs of operations that support client needs;
6. Acquisitions – direct costs of buying what the client wants as well as a proportion of the overhead costs of collections (e.g. CD-ROMs, online database subscriptions) that are indirectly related to client needs;
7. Supplies, particularly paper – photocopying and telefacsimile operations are major paper consumers;
8. Telecommunications – installation of lines, additional port connections needed, the software and hardware needed to handle the additional capacity to serve;
9. Communications and delivery – postage and couriers for physical delivery of information, correspondence, etc.;
10. Membership fees (e.g. OCLC costs to get access to shared databases and a portion of the membership fees in cooperatives, systems, and back-up resources such as the Center for Research Libraries if of benefit to the client group);
11. Administrative costs – a percentage of the time of senior administrators not directly involved in daily operations (e.g. the president or other senior officers, director of the library, finance and accounts-receivable departments of the institution; legal staff, computing center costs, MIS systems support; public relations staff and central receiving and purchasing);
12. Direct costs incurred to obtain the client's materials from external suppliers (e.g. database vendors, reprint houses, bookstores, document brokers, and libraries that charge for interlibrary loans);
13. Payment for copyright clearance for specific items or for a

proportion of membership costs for blanket clearinghouse memberships;

14. Use of a consultant to set up the service and to help with initial negotiations; and
15. Research and development costs to grow future enhancements and to evaluate and improve services.

As mentioned briefly, local policies will have to be clarified in order to identify the costs of these elements. For example, if space is to be renovated or added space is to be provided, who is responsible for that cost? Does the information supplier consider it investment capital, a capital outlay to be recovered over the first few years of operation, or directly billable to the client? Clear missions of institutions are critical. Traditional libraries that seek to carve out a role as information suppliers to those who want to outsource these services may have to re-examine their 'community service' attitudes as well as their investment strategies, and look to include support from clients. In other words, they may have to overcome a shy reluctance to look at the full potential to recover historical costs. If additional or renovated space is needed, for example, the cost burden could be jointly negotiated up-front as a shared cost between the client and the supplier.

Another policy issue that must be clarified is the proportion of indirect and historical costs that can be charged back. They could, for example, be based on any of the following:

1. A percentage of the target client group vis-à-vis the rest of the clients served;
2. A percentage of the actual or potential use of the facility or collections attributable to the client;
3. A percentage of the direct personnel costs of the whole organization.

While it would be tempting, costs should not be standardized for clients. They may vary considerably depending on the client and should remain negotiable accordingly. The organization that is seeking to establish a cost-recovery model should also pre-determine where the revenue will be credited. Will it be returned to the information service center or will all or a portion of the income go to the parent organization? For each scheme, there are also legal considerations which must be taken into account about such services and their fees. These considerations include the non-profit status of the parent institution, the tax liability of the institution, liability related to the accuracy or completeness of the information provided, the copyright clearance obligations of the organization on print- and database-oriented products, the propriety of using interlibrary loan to support fee-based information services, and the appropriate use of government documents in fee-based information services, to name a few.

Finally, there are philosophical considerations that the information service organization or its parent institution must address relating to equity of service. The philosophical arguments for these services seem to boil down to the practical observation that if information service organizations were able to contend with an increase in demand for their services by simply expanding capacity, then quantity and quality could be maintained equitably for all patrons. Fee-based services, therefore, protect the organization's ability to provide high quality services to all patrons and to offer services to a broader clientele without requiring additional funds from the general budget. Establishing fee-based services allows an organization to serve those with other options for information services (such as information brokers), but who have chosen the information service organization over their other options.

Once an organization has considered all the mission-related, economic, legal, and philosophical factors associated with the establishment of fee-based services, it should be able to weigh these considerations against the real and perceived information needs of its user community. It can then make an informed decision about its ability to provide this kind of service. Those shopping for a source from which to lease or buy information services can use the same elements to assess their best and most cost-effective alternative.

" Meeting the Demands of the Network-Linked Scholar

Instead of taking the library of the 1980s as the starting point, consider the scholar of the late 1990s: personally owned and managed computer systems are the essential tool for nearly all forms of intellectual work. In disciplines such as physics and economics – where mathematical models play an essential role – scholars develop models in their local machines, solve the problems, then explore the results, graphically. In disciplines such as literature and history –

*where the analysis of language and text has a central role —
scholars develop text databases in order to cross-index
passages or to examine the use of language in context. In a
discipline such as art or pathology — where the analysis of
images is fundamental — scholars develop archives of images,
some of them animated, in order to group related images, to
enlarge details, and to make quick comparisons between
related images. The computer workstation with an ample,
high resolution screen, significant computational power,
connected to sources of data, is the basic tool for intellectual
work in nearly every field.*

*Powerful, electronic tools are worth the investment because
they enable scholars to be more productive than conventional
tools of scholarship allow. Scholars without electronic tools
cannot compete with those who learn to use them effectively.
In disciplines where research is funded by competitively
awarded grants, scholars who do not make use of the best
tools effectively are not effective in competing for grants.
Aside from grant competition, scholars who make effective
use of electronic tools produce more work and complete
investigations of a sophistication and on a scale not possible
without these tools. Within a generation, scholars who do not
use powerful computer workstations effectively will be as
relevant to scholarship as shovel brigades are to the building
of interstate highways.*

*Scholars of the late 1990s connect their workstations to data
networks for several reasons. Networks are a convenient way
to share printers and other expensive peripherals, to establish
back-up files, and to make use of high-speed or specialized
computational services. Networks allow the sharing of data
with other scholars: a workgroup can share information so
that collaborators are working with common data. Networks
also provide a means of communication with other scholars.
Electronic mail sends simple messages around the world. (On
his NeXT computer, Steve Jobs now demonstrates more
advanced mail which allows the sender to incorporate images,
files, sound, and even video sequences in the mailgram.)
Scholars choose to link their powerful workstations to
sophisticated networks even when the local library is not a
part of one. The library, it seems, must take networks and
workstations as given.*

What library services will the network-linked scholar value? This is the pivotal question for forecasting costs for library services in the future, because institutions devoted to scholarship are unlikely to sustain the costs of services which scholars do not find to be of value. Several observations illustrate this point.

Information products delivered to the workstation via networks will be more valued than other products. Because most work will take place at the workstation, information that arrives in a form which is useful on the workstation will be worth more than information in other forms. In addition, delivery to the workstation means that the scholar will save the time associated with trips to remote locations such as libraries. And the workstation can take advantage of information products in formats such as digital sound, video, or mathematical algorithms that are otherwise not useful. For all these reasons, the network-linked scholar will place a premium on information products delivered to the workstation via the network. Information providers will have to create products that appeal to these scholars. However, such products may have higher costs than conventional information products.

The local information provider, the campus library, will lose some of its comparative advantage because remote information providers will be able to deliver information to workstations via the network about as easily as a local establishment. If journal articles are delivered to workstations by means similar to telefacsimile technology (with copyright royalties paid), the source of the transmission can be thousands of miles distant, and still deliver electronic documents with about the same speed and quality as the campus library.

A critical determinant of value will be how quickly the user needs the desired material. Information kept online can be retrieved in a few seconds by the user at a workstation. But online information is high-cost information. Alternatively, information can be kept offline but in ways that can allow delivery, say by fax, within a few hours. Or, information can be archived with requests queued so that delivery takes a few days. There is, then, a potential for a continuum of delivery speeds at graduated costs. The local library will be competing against the speed-for-a-price delivery provided by external, network-oriented, delivery services.

The charging mechanisms chosen by information providers will depend on competitive forces. The campus library, for example, will no longer have a monopoly and will therefore lose much of its discretion with respect to pricing. If online (that is, instantaneous) delivery of particular full-text materials is available at five dollars per page from remote vendors, then the local library must decide whether to offer comparable service. If it chooses to do so, its price must be less than, or equal to, the remote provider's price. If offline (overnight) delivery is available at one dollar a page, the campus library must again choose whether to offer a similar service. (These prices are approximately those offered by the British Library at Boston Spa.) No library with a substantial clientele can afford to offer full, online access or even overnight delivery – of all of its collection to all of its clients without restrictions and charges. Local libraries must offer such services or else forego the opportunity to provide significant, high-value services to its core clients. If the library chooses to offer such services, it must adopt some strategy to restrict their use so that the high costs of providing the services bear some relationship to their value to clients. In particular, the local library will want clients to decide when instant delivery (vs. overnight or several days) is worth the cost. A price structure that reflects the incremental cost of alternative modes of delivering information will work best. A library that chooses not to offer network delivery for fees, runs the risk of restricting its services to the lower-value needs of peripheral clients.

The campus library's decisions about what to collect will change remarkably. We can think of the library's purchasing priorities as a set of available items, ranked in order of value to its clients.

Conventionally, the library applied its resources well into the set to encompass quantities of material that – while not immediately needed – were likely to be of potential use. With significant delivery capabilities available from remote locations via networks, the local library may choose to purchase materials of immediate and substantial use, forgoing the accumulation of lesser-used materials because those are likely to be available as needed through the networks.

At the same time, the library may choose to develop focused collections in great depth as a means of attracting users on the international network. Unique collections, then, should become a source of revenue. The network would create broader market opportunities for strong libraries to provide information products well beyond the geographic limitations represented by their local clients.

The network-linked scholar will create a new set of demands and unleash a new set of competitive forces. Information providers must rethink their operations in light of the new opportunities and in light of the new competition. Given all these emerging conditions, the campus library will have to change drastically. **"**

Malcolm Getz

8 Shaping core services in future

- ◆ Framework for the future
- ◆ From generic to hallmark services
- ◆ Change in a no-charge culture
- ◆ Cooperation — or collaboration?

❝ The single theme that runs through the many topics raised in this chapter is how to effect change in a no-change culture. Few would deny that during the next decade external developments will have enormous impact on our libraries and information systems. These developments cannot be ignored. They are so broadly based across the scholarly community that no library can expect to remain unchanged. Yet the culture of libraries is fundamentally conservative. The training provided by library schools and the past practices of the great libraries were aimed towards building and maintaining collections over long periods. Libraries have given greater emphasis to information services, but the changes have been incremental rather than fundamental. Nothing has prepared people for the dynamic changes that many see on the horizon. **❞**

William Arms

Creating future scenarios is the game of the decade. This we will not do. We will instead try to provide a framework for defining a set of 'core' services. This framework will be grounded less in recent trends than in past and present economic, political, and social values. Extrapolating the future from past trends is particularly risky if it involves technological fields where innovations tend to take quantum leaps, not progressive ones. For this reason, we rely on others to paint pictures of what the user can expect to see in tomorrow's 'library' and concentrate instead on the strategies and elements that will enable those tomorrows to arrive and to provide a lush information environment.

Libraries of the western world have generally been referred to as information centers or information services throughout this book. Our reasons for doing this are two-fold:

1. Their prime function is the organization and dissemination of information, not education, recreation, or preservation.
2. Their future will be determined by the extent to which they succeed in creating a niche in the information chain as information distributors, in collaboration with the creators and producers.

Past practice among information workers has been to define quality as doing the best possible with as little as possible in a sweeping array of functions that include dissemination, organization, education, recreation, and the preservation of information or knowledge – all of the operations described in the early chapters of this book. The result has been like a low-grade infection. The whole organism is compromised. Peak or quality performance is impossible. Thus we argue for definition of information services that will make a significant difference by separating generic services from hallmark ones. From this definition will fall the roles to be played by various sectors in the information chain – the creators, the producers, and the providers.

“ Peering into the future is always a risky business, especially when you record what you see in print (or in some such permanent form and revisit this vision in the cold light of a later day). Nonetheless, the need to differentiate service offerings, perhaps along the lines suggested, is imperative if libraries and those who toil in them are to play a significant role in the active information sector of the future.

What form this differentiation will take is another matter and will depend very much on the particular 'world' in which an information center (or library) exists and operates. Societal objectives, goals, values, resources, and mores will have a great impact on how this differentiation takes place. There is no doubt that we cannot continue, as the authors point out, with a definition of quality that consists of doing 'the best possible with as little possible in a sweeping array of functions'. **"**

John Black

◆ Framework for the future

The underlying stimulus for change is technology. This already provides the individual with a vast choice of information sources, and offers the information industry a bewildering array of possible services. Changes in computing and communications over the next decade will have further deep impact on what is economically feasible. Although the underlying technical trends are predictable, it is impossible to forecast the ways in which cheaper and more powerful hardware will translate into improved information services. In particular, as the chapter recognizes, the economic, legal, and social frameworks which will emerge are still obscure. For example, a decade ago, engineers were able to forecast quite accurately the development of powerful personal computers, but failed to anticipate the emergence of the third-party software industry and the impact that novel applications such as desk-top publishing would have on whole professions.

" *The other driving force is financial. The 1980s were a prosperous time for higher education and the research community. Even so, libraries were hard-pressed to keep up with the increased cost of materials, the demand for computing and other electronic services, space pressure from growing collections, and the increasing range of academic specializations. Because of the general prosperity, however, it was possible to introduce new services while continuing the old. Now we are entering a time of acute financial problems for universities, the cost pressures on libraries are as great as ever, and the impetus for change is still growing. Libraries have perilously little flexibility. At least some of the funding for new initiatives will have to be found by cutting back on current activities.* **"**

William Arms

The current view among computer experts, librarians, other information professionals, publishers, and users of information is that a new order is promised by the new information technologies and new approaches to the dissemination of information. There is, however, very little consensus on either the real costs or the design elements that are needed to move to such a new paradigm. Nor are there easy paths to follow in altering the future flow of that which will guide new knowledge to its ultimate destination and be disseminated through electronic media.

There are some who believe that the costs associated with the production of information (such as the organizational structure, evaluation processes, editorial functions, etc.) are identical for both print and electronic products. Sirbu's (1991) cost-analysis research and model, described in Chapter 5, is an example of this. The Mendelian Inheritance of Man project at Johns Hopkins University (Lanier, 1990) also provides for an evaluation process on a flexible distributed system designed to transport digital information. Lanham's (1990) description of the transformation of scholarly communication to a digitally-based model is also recommended as required reading for those in higher education. Lyman (1990) has proposed a distributed economic model for publishing that would centralize the fixed costs and revenues of publishing and distribute the variable costs and revenues. He also proposes a different perspective whereby intellectual property is valued to the extent that its usefulness is enhanced. In the economic model he proposes the sharing of information would be protected by law, and activities like copying would actually be rewarded. Another perspective is presented by Weber (1991) who interviewed publishers and academicians to create scenarios, or endstates, as he calls them. His premises include the following:

- **Telephone companies prevail**. They will generate and publish information along the wires they already own.

In light of a decision by the US courts in the summer of 1991 to allow this to happen, pending conclusion of appeals, North American telephone companies appear to be developing an unshakable foundation for the future of information transfer. In Europe, where telecommunications companies such as Minitel are operated by France Telecom, a government agency, the information transfer function has already been awarded to telephone companies.

- **Computer companies prevail**. They bundle electronic publications into their machines as a means to enhance hardware sales and distribution.

This is not just a distant dream. Computer companies are already including software and text databases such as dictionaries and encyclopedias with applications software and are selling workstations that include CD-ROM or laser disks that have text, numeric, and experimental image databases as integral components.

- **Universities prevail**. They will establish the intellectual property rights of their faculty to be institutional assets and reassert their rights over intellectual property generated on campuses.

The current economic climate for higher education indicates that this premise may be questionable. If it is upheld, it could have a two-pronged result. First, all of the institutions that exist today may not survive. Closures and mergers are occurring. This trend will likely not abate until a critical mass of institutions is established that balances the demand for services. Second, it may be difficult for institutions to establish property rights over all of the intellectual output of its scholars and researchers. Most universities take the stance that they own, control, and have worldwide rights to patentable products that result from activities of their faculty, staff and students. In these instances, royalties from patents are usually split between the institution and the inventor. Royalties from literary outputs, however, traditionally have not been subjected to such stringent controls. The extension of 'literary outputs' into the electronic environment, as full-text databases or CD-ROM products (i.e. electronic information), presents a muddy policy area for higher education. Since traditions and past-precedents are relatively unshakable in academia, it may be difficult for this end-state of Weber's to be realized, let alone become a potential source of income.

“ *Historically, libraries are less successful in exercising control over the role that their own institutions play in creating information. This is particularly true in universities. University faculty form the biggest single group of academic authors. The system of rewards encourages them to publish as many papers as possible with no consideration being given to the economics of publication. Universities and their libraries will have to develop new incentives to stimulate cost-effectiveness as a criterion in the publication of research results. As a simple example, the proposal recently made by*

162

the president of Stanford University that only six papers be considered in promotion decisions would encourage faculty to put the maximum content into each paper. **"**

William Arms

Weber's final scenario is that

- **Publishers prevail**. Their added-value products will predominate in an environment where there are no better alternatives.

Given the global consolidation of media, publishing, and the information industry in general, publishers (and their parent companies) will most assuredly predominate. They have already captured most of the 'information' market and are leveraged to change and adapt it in ways that few non-profit organizations are positioned to do. Within the public sector, there have been efforts to design future models for information services but there is very little public funding available to support the needed research.[1] The result for the information service professions is that they have not made much progress toward establishing a common definition of such models, or on the economics of financing them.

" *The summary of Weber's 'endstates' is provocative and his final prognosis will be viewed as frightening by many. It may in fact be a logical outcome of current trends, but the information world does not have to develop in this fashion and other possibilities, particularly for scholarly, scientific and technical information are certainly possible. Whether agencies such as the Coalition for Networked Information in the US can provide a focus for some countervailing developments remains to be seen, but CNI's work in the context of many other networking developments does provide hope, particularly in the United States.* **"**

John Black

Recently, a Coalition for Networked Information (CNI) was formed as a joint venture between the Association of Research Libraries, CAUSE, concerned with college and university adminis-

---

[1] Designs that have had support include the IAIMS model funded by the National Library of Medicine (Matheson, 1982) and the future research library that resulted from a retreat sponsored by the Council on Library Resources (Woodsworth et al., 1989).

trative computing, and EDUCOM, an organization concerned about academic computing. The potential of CNI for North America lies in its being a forum through which common definitions, economic models, and possible solutions to information communications of all kinds can be defined. It is too soon to predict if this promise will materialize.

If information providers listen to the tempo of the corporate world today, they will hear a litany of words that are antithetical to their past practices in many respects: market niche and market creation, flat and flexible organizations, individual focus, uncompromised quality, change as a source of strength, to name a few. In a broader political context, towns, counties, and municipalities are in dire financial straits and are talking consolidation, downsizing, and merger of all of their operations, including social services. Again, these are concepts that are anathema to librarians and create almost knee-jerk protests.

“ The 'tempo of the corporate world' does indeed generate a litany of worlds and a host of concepts that are antithetical to what many librarians view as their prime mission, but that does not, per se, mean that this litany should become the primary driving force for their future direction. Other voices are speaking as well, e.g. in the university area, calling on our institutions to revisit their primary goals, and their clientele, and in the process refocus on the needs of students.

As indicated, in North America individuals are increasingly living in a 'plugged-in' world with a widening range of information sources and access to technologies. Distributed access, networks and personal information-processing technologies are the order of the day. At the same time there is a widening gap between those who fully use these facilities, technologies, and resources, and those who do not, cannot, and without great help, never will be able to do so. When one goes outside of North America and some other parts of the developed world, the information 'gap' becomes a chasm, before which all other issues in this discussion pale. **”**

John Black

At the individual level, there are more choices and more uncertainties than ever before. Radio, television, newspapers, magazines, bookstores, personal computers, telephones, and the like are all empowering individuals with information access. The systems are not necessarily mutually exclusive but they do provide more competition for traditional information providers such as libraries.

All of these factors point to the need for information centers to make choices about how they can make a difference at the individual level – in short, determine their niche in the information market more tightly and clearly. To do this requires that they do a better job of differentiating both the kinds of services provided and how well each is going to be done.

◆ From generic to hallmark services

The gamut of functions performed in most information centers was described in Chapter 2. As stated before, all of these things tend to be done with never enough money. Yes, everything gets done (oh, we might have a small cataloging backlog of a million or two). Well-intentioned, overworked and underpaid folks try to do everything as well as they can (well, it's mostly the user's mistakes that account for them finding what they want only 58 per cent of the time). Without the benefit of crystal balls, guesses are made about purchases of millions of dollars worth of books and information containers that users might want tomorrow (yes, we know that only 20 per cent of what we buy accounts for 80 per cent of what is used, but we have to preserve the other 80 per cent just in case someone needs it ten years from now). What is the result in terms of quality of information centers? It can best be pictured as an accumulation of breadcrumbs that have settled fairly uniformly into the bottom of a basket as opposed to an artfully appealing, but limited selection of fresh and exotic loaves of bread.

“ *The concept of tiered levels of service clearly highlights the realities that information centers/libraries face today and provides one potential articulation of these realities. The implementation of such tiers, however, will be much more dependent on the organizational, institutional, or community/ societal cultures than is here indicated. Again one has to be wary of slavish or inappropriate application of 'corporate models' in these areas.* **”**

John Black

To reach a definition of 'hallmark' service for any function, information centers will need to identify what areas are appropriate for 'null' service, what they deem to be 'generic' (or core) services, what their users see as 'anticipated' services, and what might be offered as 'enhanced' services. Once these definitions are in place, an organization can then draw its lines for free, subsidized, or full cost recovery as desired or howsoever local needs or policy dictate. Without this framework, funding and charging decisions are left to rest mostly on the outcome of the kinds of philosophical debates discussed in earlier chapters.

As shown in Figure 8.1, the amount invested in hallmark service

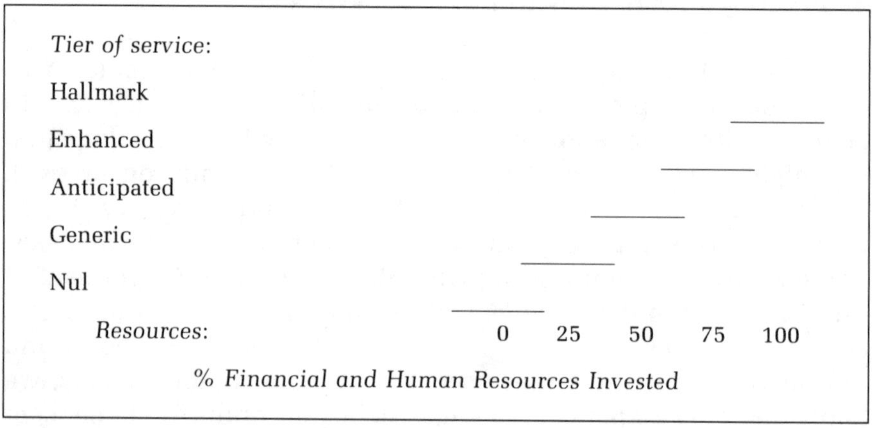

Tier of service:

Hallmark

Enhanced

Anticipated

Generic

Nul

Resources:

0   25   50   75   100

% Financial and Human Resources Invested

Figure 8.1 Tiers and resource relationships

should be based on a 'whatever it takes' philosophy. So 100 per cent of the resources needed to provide a hallmark service have to be supplied. The relative amounts invested in enhanced, anticipated, and generic services can be adjusted to suit local conditions, but they are inversely proportionate to the level of service being provided.

The crux of this model lies in defining the bottom and top ranges of the scale. The **generic** level is the absolute minimum required. This is not what information workers would like, not what users would like, but the nub that remains before doing away with the function entirely. In the business of borrowing materials from another library, for example, generic service could be defined as providing forms for users to fill out and mail to the places that designated users themselves guess to have the materials. The role of the information center would be to notify users when the items arrive. The client would be expected not only to provide verifiable information about the item but also where it can be found, all in a form that could be forwarded directly without any checking or verification for accuracy by information center staff. No additional locations would be sought if the borrower-designated sites did not work. The cheapest possible means of communication (e.g. surface mail) would be used for both requests and items.

At present, most libraries provide services at **anticipated** levels for this function. In interlibrary lending and borrowing, for example, information center staff verify the correct title, etc., of the item and find and determine the best (fastest and cheapest) places to send the request. Normally, if the location of first choice cannot supply an item, it will be forwarded to another, either by information center staff or the computer system used to facilitate inter-institutional borrowing. Requests are tracked and claimed if they do not appear in a reasonable amount of time and users are alerted about the status of their request after a reasonable period. Although materials themselves may be sent by surface mail, some may be sent by fax or courier if speed is important to the user, and/ or if they are willing to pay for faster delivery. At this level of service, resources would include some level of professional involvement to supervise support staff along with appropriate equipment such as terminal access to databases, networks and telefacsimile transmission.

Enhanced levels of service are what some libraries are now striving to give in their attempts to rely less on ownership and more on providing access to materials. At this level of service, users might experience the following when they ask for something that is not in their local collection:

- full verification of citations by information workers;
- requests for deadlines beyond which items are no longer useful;
- materials supplied within requested time limits;
- actual or facsimile copies supplied irrespective of cost or source; and
- delivery of items to the office or workplace of the requestor.

At this level, the means for transmission of requests and materials to libraries, commercial document suppliers, etc. would use state-of-the-art systems and technologies. Service would be provided by a reasonable mix of professional and clerical staff.

At the top of this continuum, the **hallmark** level of information access and delivery service is limited only by the imagination of those defining it. It could, for example, take advantage of the kinds of experimental delivery systems described in Chapter 4 and provide:

- summaries or abstracts that synthesize the materials received;
- electronic transmission of requests from users to the information center with automatic sorting and shunting through document centers and resource centers to national libraries and publishers;
- guaranteed delivery within 24 hours;
- delivery in the clients preferred format (e.g. paper copy, data files, floppy disk, or the actual artifact); and
- automatic delivery of new information, as published, about certain topics as defined in advance.

" *The proposal for hallmark services in this chapter provides a good example of the type of innovation that libraries must be able to handle. The proposal is appealing, with its assertion that there is a market for hallmark information services for which the user would pay. To introduce such a concept on even a limited basis, a library will have to invest resources in creating and marketing the service. Libraries need to become organizations in which such experiments are seen as a natural process where services are designed, tested, and allowed to flourish if successful or wound up if not. Staff need to be dedicated to the experiments, empowered to modify the plans, and willing to recognize and accept failure should it happen. Unfortunately, libraries and librarianship are not well-equipped to handle this sort of organizational innovation. New services are often seen as the last priority when all ongoing activities are completed. For these reasons, the chapter rightly emphasizes the need for library education that will impart an altered consciousness about information, and the importance of continuing education for everybody in the information chain.* **"**

William Arms

The tiered model somewhat resembles zero-based budgeting exercises, but its aim is not elimination so much as identification of an area or two in which an information center can invest heavily and on which rest the primary definition of its identity and values. The quality of hallmark services are such that they stretch the outer boundaries of the dreams of information center users. They would be operated by a team whose foremost objectives are individual service and quality. The result would be a dependency relationship with users that make both institutional and individual investments (and any fees collected) more than worthwhile.

Other services in information centers (e.g. database searching and circulation) likewise could be sorted into generic, anticipated, enhanced, and hallmark levels. Doing so would arm information professionals with the tools they need to stop doing everything at a mediocre level with the least amount of money. More importantly, if information centers can develop one or two hallmark services, their capacity to collect revenues and additional support could be enhanced to the point that they will have 'investment' capital to develop additional hallmark service. This assumes, of course, that the services are being managed properly.

Sorting out information service operations in this way will also help information professionals identify what it is they mean when they talk about 'core' services. Most libraries have tended to define core services as those that are not new and/or those for which there is no charge. Since these can vary enormously depending on the type of information center and its location, the debate about core/non-core and fee/free issues can become quite heated. This was exemplified in 1990 and 1991 by the enormous resistance mounted by the community library in the United States when the Library of Congress (LC) tried to clarify its cost recovery mechanisms for certain 'marginal' services. LC has been charging fees for decades for certain services such as buying foreign materials for other libraries or for copying print or images for commercial enterprises. At least part of the protest arose because LC's definition of core service was not universally understood. Again, as was pointed out in Chapter 7, information centers need to clearly define what they mean by 'core', 'value-added' and 'generic' services. Without such distinctions, they will continue to be misunderstood, and will correctly be perceived as not understanding themselves what they do and how they fit into an information society.

◆ Change in a no-charge culture

Information centers that want to develop hallmark services, or that want to compete with information brokers and the information industry in information delivery, will need to consider carefully how to staff those services. They must decide whether or not they can afford the time to 'grow' the staff they now have into the kinds of free-wheeling, creative, change agents that are needed, or whether they have to compete with the private sector and hire them fully grown.

In the hallmark, or even the enhanced, models of information services, the organizational and individual cultures and styles needed are not always a comfortable fit for traditional information professionals. To wit, Nordstrom's department store, renowned for its hallmark service orientation, has its personnel on the floor anticipating questions and needs. Most libraries do not do this. If they do, the barriers built against client contact can be formidable: for example, information service desks that are out of sight; employees not identified; employees always seeming to be busy doing other things; telephones with several lines ringing and pre-empting personal assistance; and vast spaces (floors and rows of book collections) with no employee presence at all.

Another factor, alluded to earlier, that makes a significant difference between generic and hallmark services, is the providing of assistance to clients to help them to determine the value of the panoply of information they get. A quality bookstore employee, for example, will help a buyer determine which tax-preparation handbook is most suitable. A librarian will help by finding an array of books but will stop giving assistance at the point when the client asks which is best. The document delivery firm that consistently provides value-added and speedy service will get return business from clients. Libraries will lose those clients (and potential revenues) unless they can compete with the same quality, level, and speed of service.

For these reasons, information workers will have to change what they do along with their ethos, including the values they place on speed and income generation. Information centers that have healthy and vibrant bottom lines will need managers with new orientations along these lines. Since both corporate and academic campuses are creating chief information officers (CIOs) to manage all aspects of information resources and systems, it is natural to assume that the people filling these positions have the appropriate 'take charge' characteristics. Also, because CIOs have more money at risk than the traditional library or computing center directors, they are more likely to be conscious of the need for quality of

170

output and speed of delivery. In the wired world, information resources have a high degree of visibility. If a data network is down, almost all work grinds to a halt. If information centers and functions of other operations in an organization are symbiotically inter-dependent, then the information service network cannot be eliminated. What remains then is for information workers to change their culture to one that gives more recognition to the bottom line of their operations – to take a 'charge' stance in all senses of the word.

The move from ownership to access, on the other hand, is one tendency that will prevail and in the process will dramatically affect libraries, their staff, their clients, and their owners'/funding agencies. Some of those effects are indicated in this chapter and others will include changes in cost allocation and 'charges' in academic programs (in educational settings), and in the preservation of the intellectual record of society. Nonetheless, a strong argument can be made to move libraries, especially research and special libraries, from the classic 'just in case' model of collection building to the 'just in time' model for quick access to specific units of information as/when required.

" As we move from ownership to access, 'payment' for the information provided by these new arrangements raises some practical and philosophical questions. In a traditional library, the user (be he/she an undergraduate student or public library user) normally does not pay directly to consult materials such as books, journals, indices, abstracts, or even CD-ROM databases. If such materials are now obtained via 'access' arrangements from commercial suppliers, for example, will the cost burden be shifted and, if so, in what way? By this relatively straightforward and completely logical change in direction, libraries may in fact dramatically alter the way in which large numbers of existing users get access to information. "

John Black

If the access model prevails, as we suspect it will in most libraries, information workers will need to learn to manage change, not stability, and will have to alter the bases of their self-esteem. They will have to devalue collections, size of the organization, and physical facilities. Their values systems will have instead to be grounded in their ability to forecast information needs, to navigate the world's electronic network, and to treasure lack of permanence in work and organizational structures. Leaders will have to appreciate the differences between managing access and managing resources.

All of these factors speak to the changes needed in the management capacities of existing and future information workers – to ensure a cadre who are able to use analytic tools along with intuition. This necessitates an increase in the amount of time and money invested in staff training and development, as well as changes in formal education. A basic role that must be assumed by schools which educate information professionals (computing and information science, librarianship and telecommunications) is to turn out students who have an altered consciousness about information creation, production, and dissemination.

" If the library profession and its schools are to thrive over the next few years, they will have to put greater emphasis on the management of change. Traditionally, libraries have altered little over the years. The management structures which have developed are those that work well in stable organizations, with hierarchical reporting, structured decision-making, and centralized financial control. Little emphasis has been given to flexibility, experimentation, and opportunistic management. It is, for example, common to find a university library with a budget of tens of millions of dollars and several hundred employees, that has no budget for innovation. One of the nation's richest libraries had such an inflexible budget that it could not buy a Macintosh computer for its new director! "

William Arms

Since information workers are more than just those with formal education in the field, one of the growth areas for schools of library and information studies lies in preparing professionals in other fields to function in the information chain – as indexers or database designers in special disciplines, for example. Another source of help for the change process is in the information industry itself. Private companies invest a substantial amount in the training and development field and many offer workshops and seminars to the public at large. It is not difficult to imagine the potential benefits in having training and education programs mounted collaboratively by a university, a publishing giant, and a computer manufacturer.

◆ Cooperation – or collaboration?

Among the information professions, libraries in particular have prided themselves on having a lengthy history of cooperative enterprises among their own kind. The Research Libraries Group, and OCLC are sterling examples. In the future showdown between profit and non-profit information providers, however, traditional information centers will have to look outside this familiar setting.

Collaboration between complementary enterprises to enhance service and products have become almost a distinguishing characteristic of growth and success in the private sector. Within the information industry, there are signs that collaboration is spanning the profit and non-profit sectors. Some universities and colleges are forging links with companies that enrich the capacities of both partners – through pure and applied research, education, and product development.

66 In recent years, leading libraries and information services have attempted to exert more control over the environment within which they operate. Perhaps the most successful current example is the emerging cooperation between libraries and academic publishers which has been fostered by organizations such as the Society for Scholarly Publishing and the Coalition for Networked Information. Libraries and publishers have many common interests and are subject to many of the same pressures, yet the relationship between them is often unduly antagonistic. Both will benefit from an orderly market for electronic information. As an example, several publishers, including UMI, Elsevier, and the American Chemical Society are currently working with universities to experiment with electronic versions of current journals. 99

William Arms

This trend begs a question about which information functions will benefit most from collaborative work and which will best be managed through non-collaborative means. From the point of view of improving their knowledge of operational effectiveness, information access and retrieval systems developers (and users) would benefit enormously from alliances with MIS (Management Information Systems) vendors. Collaboration on the development of standards for all aspects of the information business is occurring but could be hastened and would be of benefit to information resources users. It would also improve the marketability of products. To provide seamless access to information, information professionals will need to work with the producers of machines and systems, who design the electronic networks, databases, and search engines.

To date, the costs of building databases for use on a global basis have been distributed throughout both private and public sectors. Again, collaboration among these actors in the information chain can be of benefit to both sellers and buyers of information. Libraries have daily contact with users in search of information. They could profitably collaborate with publishers to develop the products and containers that respond to needs, rather than both trying to anticipate what the market will want.

Collaboration between commercial document delivery firms and resource rich libraries also has win–win potential. In this kind of alliance, large research libraries could provide the pools from which the distributors (such as UMI and Faxon) draw their documents. From the point of view of suppliers, they avoid the cost of building collections and housing them. At the same time, the research libraries can use the revenue generated from being document-suppliers to further enrich their ability to provide information services. Similarly, if there are limits to what vendors will want to store and archive, libraries could become the historical repositories (as well as the supplying collaborators) for vendors.[2]

" Collaboration with the 'commercial' sector has many
attractive features, particularly if this collaboration results in
a positive cash flow for the library involved. For example, it
is suggested that 'collaboration between commercial document
delivery firms and research rich libraries has win–win
potential' especially for large research libraries. It can also be
argued, however, that such arrangements may have very
negative impacts on many other libraries and may place

---

[2] The possibility that a limited number of research libraries will eventually emerge to fulfill this type of role is more fully discussed in the article by Woodsworth et al., 1988).

174

many long-standing cooperative ventures at risk. At a time when technological opportunities would deliver control of their information destiny back to universities, as indicated by Weber's 'endstates', this collaboration with the commercial sector could well have exactly the opposite effect. **"**

John Black

Another collaborative enterprise that would benefit information seekers would be for their libraries to work with book stores, book-jobbers, and publishers so that lists and inventories are available through either local information systems or external networks. Information seekers could then, when they find something they want, decide whether to borrow it or buy it. Given an easy ordering and delivery system, this kind of marketing access could well improve sales for vendors and would certainly make the information system more friendly to users. Both collaborators in this kind of enterprise would need to have dynamic and coordinated delivery systems. Newer technological developments, such as artificial intelligence and expert systems, expand those possibilities into areas such as the translation of works in various languages or the provision of guides that get network travellers to their destinations.

The potential for collaboration is virtually endless. All that is needed is for a few visionaries from the information service sector to connect with their counterparts in a complementary part of the commercial sector. If money speaks, then take-charge information professionals will be able to influence information producers and their markets. The commercial information sector understands that competitive advantage is not necessarily based on having a basic product, but rather on the differences (the bells and whistles) that make it stand out in the pack. Since information centers do and will pay for quality products, it behoves them to work with the information providers to ensure that the intellectual content remains relevant.

◆ A final word

" Yes, people expect to pay for service, but in many settings this concept will disenfranchise those who need access to

these services the most – college and university students, members of the public who do not have the economic resources to allocate to information access, or even small business/research groups without the resources of their large corporate (or governmental) counterparts. Keying the differentiation of service to the ability to pay will perhaps allow for the enhancement of service to some and provide some tangible indicators of success. But the social cost will be deemed unacceptable to many. **"**

John Black

People will pay for hallmark information services irrespective of who the providers are – the private sector or publicly funded libraries. People are increasingly reluctant to pay (whether through their taxes, or on a cash basis) for services and products that are generic. The better packaged product sells. So do products from manufacturers who have shed the value of planned obsolescence. People expect to pay for services. But they will not pay a second time if the services are not prompt and on target. People *will* pay more for quality. How much more this might be in the information environment, will depend on whether hallmark, enhanced, anticipated, or generic services are being provided.

Therefore, information service professionals must take charge of identifying their primary market niche, creating suitable hallmark services, and then charging accordingly. Pieces of information operations that do not contribute to setting a center apart from other information providers must either be abandoned or reduced to generic levels. At this lower end of the scale, outsourcing is a good tactic for information centers. At the upper end, the information centers have the potential to be the places to which other organizations turn for outsourcing.

" *Perhaps the greatest difficulty of all in this time of experimentation will be to maintain balance. Throughout the scholarly community there has long been a deep respect for the value that a good library provides and a willingness to support it. (Carnegie Mellon is a rare example of a university which has prospered by, quite deliberately, restricting funds for the libraries, while investing heavily in other facilities, notably computing.) In many universities, the library building* *occupies the most imposing location on campus and its architecture symbolizes the commitment to scholarship. This symbolic role creates a situation where attention to the past can become a barrier to the future. More modern thinking emphasizes the scholar as a consumer and information as a consumer product, but this way of thinking is still evolving. Mistakes will be made. Not all new ideas withstand the test of time. The best information services of the future surely will combine the traditions of the old with the vitality of the new. To do this at a time of financial stringency is a challenge for us all.* **"**

William Arms

The following comments are both from the perspective of higher education environments. The first is from Maurice Glicksman:

" *O'Neill (1981) has observed that authors looking at the future have tended to make two errors. In his words, 'most prophets have overestimated how much the world would be transformed by social and political change and underestimated the forces of technological change'. The authors try to avoid such pitfalls by concentrating on the 'strategies and elements' that libraries (information services or centers) should employ to facilitate their future development, and leave to others the 'paint[ing of] pictures of what the user can expect to see'. The authors have provided an interesting but limited perspective for guiding the future of those information services. They suggest an apparently rational approach to rationing resources, with no guidance as to which services to apply it to and how to come to the decisions on relative priorities – other than to employ a good bottom-line oriented manager and to consider setting appropriate charges to support the exceptional service. They also have not avoided the trap O'Neill noted, as suggested below.*

I take a university perspective on information services. I view the university as providing three services to society: the creation of knowledge, the communication of knowledge and the conservation of knowledge (Glicksman, 1987), and I expect the university's information services to contribute to these three goals, to the first as a supporter and to the second and third as a major partner. This chapter does not accept all of these as priorities for the information services function; indeed it confines the libraries to the organization and dissemination of information, omitting the conservation ('preservation') to which I would give comparable priority.

What the authors do is to note that information services are currently over-extended and will be even more so in the future. Hence the future requires that, even more than in the present, services will have to be rationed. The amount of rationing will depend on the particular service and the institution's priorities. But the information center is advised to decide that some services will not be provided at all, that others will be provided at various levels from minimal ('generic') through anticipated and enhanced levels to the desirable but rarely feasible level of 'hallmark'. In the last case, essentially 100 per cent of the resources necessary to provide the best service will be dedicated to this service, with unlimited application of service and technology to that end. And the information center will charge appropriate prices for providing such quality services. The authors contend that the market will pay those extra prices, although they fail to tell us which services will satisfy this description and where the market is for them.

The authors note that the situation calls for cooperation and collaboration, including the real sharing of resources to ensure the best service for the information center's customers. They are not optimistic, however, that libraries and information centers will be able to give up the autonomy needed for real sharing leading to cost saving.[3] As is pointed out, OCLC and the Research Libraries Group are examples of successful cooperative ventures, and there are proposals that the organizational framework so formed could be used for cooperation over a broader range of services, to enhance quality at the lowest possible cost. But recent efforts to have those two organizations cooperate more fully in exploring this broader application of the cooperative, collaborative principle have failed. Network development offers a possible vehicle for better cooperation in the delivery of information.

However, there are both profit-making and non-profit organizations in the information business. There is the

---

[3] See Glicksman (1985) for a similar view.

political and economic principle that is written into American law that requires competition in commerce and not collaboration, since the latter is believed to stifle competition and cause inflated prices. This may ultimately limit the level of cooperation in providing services, even if the individual institutions become convinced that they must give up some autonomy to provide the services at the level they wish to, or at the level which allows them to survive.

Although there are a few commercial libraries, and there may be more commercial information centers in the future, history has provided us with evidence that the 'commercial' libraries of the past were unable to provide sufficiently broad services to the bulk of the population at prices which fit the perceived need. Instead, our society has decided that information is so important to it that it provides direct and indirect public support to assure an economically and politically strong nation.

The authors have actually proposed a future scenario they apparently wanted to avoid. The proposal to provide highest quality services through the charge route leads to a societal change: realistic charges for information services hitherto provided at highly subsidized prices. This is not a technological change which is proposed, but rather a bold social one. My comment above about the absence of evidence for the authors' statement that such services can be provided in an appropriate market niche, and that there are customers who can and will pay for them, is pertinent here. Without knowing where these customers are, what the service is and what the order of magnitude of the expected price would be, it is hard to judge the viability of this approach.

I recall a proposal I made to a large information services audience for a realistic charging approach in providing quality computing resources (Glicksman, 1984). Many in the audience reacted as though I had proposed repealing one of the Ten Commandments. The discussion that followed was emotional. A feeble attempt I made later to implement such an approach failed to educate the users to the costs – one of its goals – and crippled those users least able to bear those costs. The niche of rich users was not there. Those most hurt were the students using the computer to write their theses, and the charging experiment was quickly terminated.

The reader needs to have good examples before such an approach can be considered seriously.

The proposal that we need to choose into which services we put our resources is a good one. But we need to recognize that recovering large investments in certain services through appropriate charges may not be as viable a solution for information services as it may be for automobiles, computer systems, and other products. Transportation services have gone through the technological fallout (with airplanes/airports and autos/superhighways cutting much out of the market held by the railroads/rail-lines/stations in our country). The hallmark service provided by the supersonic Concorde failed to generate more than a very small market niche, subsidized to enable it to exist at all. The commercial players (publishers, communications companies, network agencies, etc.) in the field will help test that approach best, and it may be most prudent for the libraries to let them test the waters and find the kinds of 'niches' the authors have in mind. In the meantime, the informations services/libraries have to provide the basic services to their organizations to enable them to function effectively in an increasingly difficult economic climate, and to do so with full attention to the costs and benefits of the use of technology. **"**

The next comment is by David A. Hoekema:

" How can librarians, scholars, and administrators cooperate to ensure responsible and effective use of emerging technologies for purposes of research and communication? How much help do libraries owe their users in gaining access to relevant research materials? Questions such as these underlie the strategies for the planning and provision of services to library users discussed in this provocative chapter.

Many pitfalls lurk for the unwary, including difficulties both of communication and of organization on campus. The degree of cooperation between library administrators and faculty members on most campuses is far higher than it was a decade or two ago, yet misunderstandings persist. As libraries take up new technologies such as online database access, CD-ROM reference material and electronic text transfer, close cooperation with data services administrators is equally necessary but much less common. University computer operations are commonly separated both financially and administratively from library operations and general faculty research support. As a result, these three communities may never come together to articulate common goals and coordinate efforts to achieve them.

Members of all three communities on campus, moreover, can be seduced by the dazzle of new technologies to value innovation over long-range effectiveness. Consider as an example the enormous expansion of CD-ROM use in libraries in the past year or two. The compactness and ease of installation of CD-ROM readers, unfortunately, cannot make up for their inherent limitation to one user at a time (except in a network system) or the difficulty of remote access. Tape loading of the same data onto a mainframe – to all appearances an outdated and more cumbersome technology – actually offers more convenient access to more users and, potentially, better integration with other databases and catalog records.

At my university, for example, I am able to log onto a mainframe via a modem and use several database services, including the library catalog and a few business and general databases, from my office or my home. But to consult the bibliographic sources I use most often in my research (apart from the Philosopher's Index, which my library has only in printed form) I must walk to the library and, except in the infrequent occasions when the CD-ROM reader happens to be unused, I must sign up to reserve a time later in the day when I can access the information.

Perhaps CD-ROM disks will prove to be the delivery vehicle of choice for low-use reference materials, while other technologies bear the burden of high-use services. But libraries that have invested heavily in CD-ROM disks and readers may find that, in their eagerness to embrace an intriguing new technology, they have become wedded to a system that does not fully meet user needs.

We must keep in mind that the library is not really a collection of information. Rather, it is a collection of research materials and of tools for access and interpretation of those materials. The question of what level of service libraries should offer is a question of how much of its effort and its budget should be expended on tools – including staff time –

that facilitate the use of its collection; that attempt, as it were, to meet users halfway and lead them to resources that will be useful for their research goals.

A bare minimum level of service – a hypothetical bare-bones library – might contain nothing more than the shelf stacks, the card catalog, and a few circulation clerks and door guards. The staff's response to every question would be, 'I don't know, I only work here'. (Remember, this is a hypothetical example, and any resemblance to any existing library is purely coincidental.) Users would be completely on their own in locating relevant material.

The opposite extreme, the highest level of service, is represented – not hypothetically – in some special-purpose corporate or law libraries, where a staff with extensive specialized training is willing to conduct nearly every stage of research and present the results to the library's users. Users sit down with a librarian to describe the information they need, and an hour or a day later the librarian delivers the relevant photocopies and summaries.

College and university libraries, needless to say, fall somewhere in the middle of this continuum. Hence the central questions posed by Williams and Woodsworth: how much ought the library to provide in the way of assistance to users? How much more than shelves and a catalog – or, in their example, a stack of interlibrary loan forms – do libraries owe to their users?

The answer that they offer is this: libraries ought to aim high and strive to provide as much assistance as possible, and they ought to cultivate new income sources such as user fees from commercial data distributors in order to support greatly expanded services. The stated goals, the management structure, and the staff training of university libraries must all be drastically revamped in order to create an effective network of public–private collaboration, exchanging the information that the private sector needs for the cash that the libraries need.

I have several misgivings about this optimistic scenario. We need to ask not only what services should be offered but also to whom. To propose substantial expansion of services, supported by expanded user fees, is an entirely different prospect if the intended user is a corporation eager to buy business data than if the user is a graduate student working on a dissertation. The latter is completely dependent on the university's research collection and services, but one cannot realistically propose to demand stiff fees for every service provided to him or her.

The source of new revenue requires careful consideration, as does the competitive position of the university library with relation to other potential information sources. Perhaps some expanded services could generate new revenues within the university structure. Departments and individual faculty members might be willing to pay $25 per citation for a rapid article search and overnight full-text delivery, for example. But to rely on such income sources does not solve any financial problems of the university. It simply shifts them from the librarian's budget to someone else's. Only new fees attracted from outside the university should be counted as genuinely new revenue sources for expanded services.

Moreover, a library that succeeds in building its staff and user services on the basis of new user fees must always be prepared to lose its newly-won business to a competitor. That is precisely the origin, after all, of existing commercial data distributors. The universities (and some industrial laboratories) pioneered both the idea and the technology of electronic data exchange. It proved so successful and so useful that commercial enterprises stepped in, using economies of scale to offer users better services at an attractive cost while turning a profit. University libraries have few competitors as repositories of research material across the whole range of scientific and scholarly endeavor. But in the much narrower domain of information needed by commercial users, competition could arise quickly.

Imagine a concrete example. Suppose a university library has laboriously built just the sort of close public–private collaboration that Williams and Woodsworth envisage. Its budget problems are long forgotten. A highly motivated and technically adept staff, and a vigorous acquisition program in both print and electronic materials, are all supported by user fees from commercial document delivery and information distribution firms. But now suppose that one of these firms, with an eye on its dwindling profits and heavy operating costs, announces that, as of next week, it will take over all of the information retrieval tasks now hired from the university library. What is more, it will provide the same services to anyone who wants them, at 25 per cent less than the university's charges.

In the short run, as the library's major revenue source quickly disappears, the result will be a catastrophe for the university library, and for the university. Staff cuts, service cutbacks, and other operational reductions will affect students, faculty, and outside users alike.

In the long run, any number of results are possible. Perhaps the commercial firm has underestimated its operating costs or simply cannot collect equally good information sources, and it will soon be forced to raise prices or go bankrupt. Perhaps the university can keep some of its customers by offering some services that the commercial competitor cannot match. The university library has the advantage that its income is protected from taxation. But it also bears the competitive burden of an obligation to a large population of on-campus users who are not in a position to provide substantial new revenues. Unfortunately, it is precisely those users who are likely to suffer the most if a library suffers such an unexpected reversal.

I am neither an economist nor a prophet, and I make no claim that the scenario I imagine is more or less likely than a situation of fruitful and sustained public–private cooperation. My point is simply this: to undertake expanded library services in the way suggested by Williams and Woodsworth opens new possibilities but also new dangers for nonprofit libraries. Are the benefits worth the risks? That is a question for others wiser than me to answer – and for all of us to ask persistently, at every stage, as we work together to adapt library collections and services to new research materials and tools. **"**

Contributors

William Y. Arms is Vice-President for Academic Services at Carnegie Mellon University with responsibility for campus computing, libraries, communications, and media. His work at Carnegie Mellon has included overseeing the development of the Andrew computer network, and he is one of the principals of the Mercury electronic library. He is a former chairman of the board of trustees of EDUCOM and is currently a member of the steering committee for the Coalition for Networked Information (CNI). His academic background is in the application of operational research and computing to libraries.

Harold Billings is Director of General Libraries at the University of Texas at Austin. Recent publications on the economics of the information flow, the organization of knowledge, and the transformation of libraries have included 'The Bionic Library' in *Library Journal* (October 15, 1991) and 'Magic and Hypersystems: A New Orderliness for Libraries' also in *Library Journal* (April 1, 1990). He has been active on many boards of directors including the Association of Research Libraries and the Center for Research Libraries in the US and is at work on an article dealing with new alliances in the information age.

John Black is Chief Librarian at the University of Guelph, Ontario, Canada. A journalist turned political scientist who has been a library administrator for two decades, he has been involved in a wide range of innovative applications of information technology in libraries, including networking, library automation, microcomputer-based information systems, CD-ROM, e-mail, and computer conferencing. He has worked extensively on international projects in China, the Pacific Rim, Africa and the Caribbean.

Jane Burke is President of NOTIS Systems, Inc., headquartered in Evanston, Illinois and a subsidiary of Ameritech Information Systems. She originally joined the staff of Northwestern University Library, the original creator of NOTIS, in 1983 as director. Under her direction NOTIS was incorporated as a for-profit organization, moved out of the academic environment, and increased its customer base from 10 to over 150. From 1977 to 1983 Burke was employed by CL Systems, Inc. (CLSI) as Central Regional Manager responsible for marketing in seventeen states. She obtained her library science degree from Rosary College in 1973 and the MBA from Northwestern University's Kellogg Graduate School of Management in 1985.

Carole Cotton, founder of CCA Consulting, has 20 years of sales and marketing management experience in a broad spectrum of high technology fields. Previous responsibilities have included: managing the North American sales and customer service operations of a $300 MM semiconductor equipment manufacturer; National Sales Manager for a robotic systems company; Regional Manager for a factory automation firm; and Marketing Manager for a library automation company. She was educated at Wellesley College and Harvard's Graduate School of Business Administration in Massachusetts.

W. Michael Cowley is CEO of Cowley & Associates, a consulting firm specializing in innovative leadership. He has held a number of management positions within the Eastman Kodak Company, including Director of Information Systems Architecture Development, Director of Information and Computing Technologies Division, Director of Research, Corporate Director of Information Technology Management and Director of Management Information Systems, Photographic Products Group. Cowley is a frequent seminar speaker on innovative information systems and has been a member of the Sponsors Board of the Center for Information Systems Research at the Massachusetts Institute of Technology.

Robert B. Croneberger has been a library administrator for 30 years, at the Library of Congress, and in the public libraries of Detroit, Michigan and Memphis, Tennessee, and now as Director of The Carnegie Library of Pittsburgh. He is an adjunct faculty member at the University of Pittsburgh's School of Library and Information Science. He has served on a number of committees of the American Library Association including its Committee on Accreditation and the Intellectual Freedom Committee. He is opposed to fees of any sort in public libraries.

Kenneth E. Dowlin, City Librarian of the San Francisco Public Library since 1987, has earned an international reputation for leadership, particularly through the creation of a world-class automated library system and the public library building programs that he has directed. From 1964 until 1987, Dowlin was director at the Arvada Public Library in Colorado, the Natrona County Public Library in Wyoming, and the Pikes Peak Library District in Colorado. He has contributed to six different books, authored over 40 articles and a widely read book, *The Electronic Library*, published in 1984. Dowlin has served in numerous professional associations, is past president of the Library and Information Technology Association in the US and has the MA in Library Science from the University of Denver and the MA in Public Administration from the University of Colorado at Colorado Springs.

Malcolm Getz has been a faculty member in economics at Vanderbilt University since 1973. In 1984 he became Director of The Jean and Alexander Heard Library, which includes the collections and facilities of all the University Libraries. Getz has been Associate Provost for Information Services and Technology since 1985, responsible for the Heard Library, the Computer Center and initiatives in academic computing. He earned his BA in economics from Williams College and his PhD in economics from Yale University. He is the recipient of a Woodrow Wilson Fellowship, a Southern Fellowship, and a National Science Foundation Fellowship. Getz's recent writing addresses economic issues in libraries, academic computing, computing in instruction, and information storage.

Maurice Glicksman is University Professor and Professor of Engineering and Physics at Brown University where for twelve years he served as Provost. He has been Chairman of the Board of the Center for Research Libraries and a member of the Higher Education Policy Advisory Committee to OCLC. He earned his PhD from the University of Chicago in Physics and his research and publications have been mainly in that discipline. He is also the author of 'Supporting Scholarship in Universities: A Response to the Growing Cost of Information Services' in *Financing Information Services* (Greenwood, 1985) and 'Changing Patterns of Scholarly Communication: Implications for Libraries' in *Library Acquisitions: Practice and Theory* **14** (1990).

Morris Goldstein is President of the Information Access Group headquartered in Foster City, California. Information Access is a division of Ziff Communications and is the world's leading supplier of electronically published periodical reference products. Goldstein serves in many capacities in the Information Industry Association and other organizations both nationally and internationally. He has twice been keynote speaker at conferences presented by the National Conventions of Online, Inc. He presented and published 'The Year 2000', in *Information Services & Use* (1990). Goldstein holds a BS from Carnegie Tech and an MBA from the Wharton School of Business.

Robert M. Hayes is Emeritus (Professor and Dean) at the Graduate School of Library and Information Science, UCLA. He received his PhD in Mathematics from UCLA. From 1949 until joining the faculty of GSLIS/UCLA in 1964, he worked in government and industry, founding Advanced Information Systems, a company that developed computer programs for file management. Hayes has experience in business, computers, academic administration, teaching and research, and has achieved international recognition for his seminal work in information science. He has published widely, including the basic texts *Information Storage and Retrieval* (1963) and *Handbook of Data Processing for Libraries* (1970), published by John Wiley.

David A. Hoekema, Executive Director of the American Philosophical Association and Assistant Professor of Philosophy at the University of Delaware, is the author of two books *Rights and Wrongs: Coercion, Punishment and the State* (Susquehanna University Press, 1986) and *Student Life and Moral Community: In*

Place of Loco Parentis (Rowman and Littlefield, In press). He has written numerous articles on topics in political philosophy, ethics, the philosophy of art, social implications of technology, and higher education and has spoken frequently on information needs and technology at associations of scholars and librarians. He serves on the National Advisory Council of the Commission on Preservation and Access and the Board of Directors of the National Humanities Alliance in the US.

Richard Rowe, is President and CEO of the Faxon Company, a $400 million multi-national company based in Westwood, Massachusetts. Under his leadership the company developed LINX, an online network which links sources and users of information. Prior to joining Faxon in 1979, Rowe was Director of the Cambridge office of the American Institute of Research, which he founded in 1973. Prior to that, he was Associate Dean of the Harvard Graduate School of Education and Director of the program in Clinical Psychology and Public Practise. Rowe is active in child and family welfare policy issues at state and national levels, has served as Chairman and President of the Statewide Advisory Council to the Office for Children in Massachusetts, and currently serves on the Massachusetts State Board of Education. His PhD in psychology is from Columbia University.

Ward Shaw is founding Chairman and CEO of CARL Systems. He served as Executive Director of Colorado Alliance of Research Libraries from its inception through 1991, and was responsible for creation and expansion of The CARL System. Prior to moving to CARL, he was Associate Director of Libraries at the University of Denver and at Colby College in Waterville, Maine. Shaw is a recognized expert on information systems and has lectured and written frequently on the topic. Shaw serves on the Network Advisory Committee of the Library of Congress, representing the American Society for Information Science. He has been honored by the American Library Association Library and Information Technology Association for his contributions to the field, and by the University of Northern Colorado, by which he was awarded an honorary doctorate. Shaw holds degrees from Hamilton College and Simmons College in Boston.

K. Wayne Smith is President and CEO of the Online Computer

Library Center, Inc. (OCLC), a non-profit organization whose complex computer network links 14 000 libraries in 46 countries. His 30 years' career includes key posts in higher education, business, and government, including serving as CEO of World Book, Inc., Group Managing Partner at Coopers & Lybrand, Director of Program Analysis at the National Security Council, and University Professor at Wake Forest University. He has written and lectured extensively on systems analysis, planning, management, and using computer networks and databases to further access to the world's information. He holds a BA in political science from Wake Forest University and a PhD in political science from Princeton University.

Elsie Stephens received her doctorate from the University of Pittsburgh and has worked in schools, the information industry, corporate information centers, and colleges and universities. She is currently Dean of University Library Services at Virginia State University at Petersburg, VA. Prior to that she was Director of The Information Exchange at the Travelers Companies in Hartford, Connecticut. Her main research interest is in the application and use of information technologies.

Lois M. Warren holds an MS from Simmons College Graduate School of Library and Information Science. She began a 'traditional' career in university and government libraries and teaching library technicians at a community college. Her non-traditional career evolved since 1972 as district manager and library consultant to a US database producer, Western Canadian manager of two major US online services, and then as founder of two information brokerage/consulting companies: L.M. Warren, Inc. in 1979 and Inside Information in 1989. Her companies serve professional, academic, legal, and government clients, the corporate community, and librarians and fellow information science brokers.

James F. Williams, II has been Dean of Libraries at the University of Colorado at Boulder since 1988. His career includes 13 years as Medical Librarian and 11 years in research library administration. His research interests include health sciences librarianship, strategic planning, collection development, leadership in research libraries, and academic library resource sharing and networking. He has been a member of the Board of Regents of the National

190

Library of Medicine in the US and a Visiting Scholar and Senior Fellow at UCLA's Graduate School of Library and Information Science.

Anne Woodsworth, Dean of the Palmer School of Library and Information Science at Long Island University, New York, has a PhD in higher education administration from the University of Pittsburgh, a master's degree in library science from the University of Toronto and a BFA from the University of Manitoba, Canada. Most of her career was spent in management positions such as Associate Provost and Director of University Libraries at the University of Pittsburgh and Director of Libraries, York University in Toronto. She is a former president of the Association of Research Libraries in the US and the Canadian Association of Research Libraries. Her recent writing focuses on the ways that technologies are altering information services, organizations and work. Her most recent books are *Patterns and Options for Managing Information Technology on Campus* (American Library Association, 1991) and *Library Cooperation and Networking: A Basic Reader* (Neal-Schuman, 1991).

List of abbreviations

BITNET	Because It's Time NETwork
CAS	Chemical Abstracts Service
CAUSE	College and University Systems Exchange
CD	Compact Disk
CD-ROM	Compact Disk-Read Only Memory
CEO	Chief Executive Officer
CIO	Chief Information Officer
CNI	Coalition for Networked Information
EARN	European Academic Research Network
EDI	Electronic Data Interchange
EDUCOM	Educational Communications (association)
EDUNET	Educational Network
EFT	Electronic Fund Transfer
LAN	Local Area Network
LC	Library of Congress, USA
MARC	MAchine Readable Cataloging
MERIT	Michigan Education and Research
MILNET	Military Network
MIS	Management Information System
NREN	National Research and Education Network, USA
RFI	Request for Information
RFP	Request for Proposal
SEC	Securities Exchange Commission, USA
NSFNET	National Science Foundation Network
OCLC	Online Computer Library Center
RLG	Research Libraries Group
RLIN	Research Libraries Information Network
STI	Scientific and Technical Information
WLN	Western Library Network, USA

Bibliography

'Affording a staff' (1990), *Pace Pages*, May, 1, 21.

Allen, N. and Williams, J.F., II (1990), 'Potential impacts of the National Research and Education Network on research libraries and the scholarly community', in *Managing Information Technology: Facing the Issues, Proceedings of the CAUSE 1989 conference*. Boulder, CO: CAUSE, 357–366.

Ardis, S. and Croneis, K.S. (1987), 'Document delivery, cost containment and serial ownership', *College & Research Libraries News*, **48**, 624–627.

'Ariel: The document delivery systems that outfaxes the fax' (1991), *Research Libraries Group News*, Fall, 7.

Ascher, K. (1987), *The Politics of Privatisation: Contracting out Public Services*, New York: St. Martin's.

Association of Research Libraries (1990), *ARL Newsletter*, November, No. 153.

Boorstin, D.J. (1983), *The discovers*, New York: Random House.

Brumm, E. (1988), CIOs are no longer middle managers. *Information Week*, October 10, 68.

Byrne, S. (1986), 'Guidelines for contracting microfilming services', *Microform Review*, **15**(4), 253–264.

Cavinato, J. (1988), 'How to calculate the cost of outsourcing', *Distribution*, **87**(1), 72–74.

Clermont, P. (1991), 'Outsourcing without guilt', *Computerworld*, September 9, 67–68.

Coffman, S. and Josephine, H. (1991), 'Doing it for money', *Library Journal*, October 15, 32–36.

Dalton, M.L. (1991), 'Does anybody have a map? Accessing information in the Internet's virtual library', *Electronic Networking*, **1**(1), 31–39.

DeGennaro, R. (1985), 'Integrated online library systems: Perspectives, perceptions and practicalities', *Library Journal*, February 1, 37–40.

DeGennaro, R. (1989), 'Technology and access in an enterprise society', *Library Journal*, October 1, 40–43.

Eiblum, P. (1991), 'The broker: An integral part of the information chain', *Information Today*, **8**(9), 16–17.

University Library System (1986), *End User Searching: An Experiment at the University of Pittsburgh*, Pittsburgh, PA.

Epstein, S.B. (1991), 'Streamlining costs with technology', *Library Journal*, May 15, 62–64.

Faxon (1991), 'Client communication update: Electronic Data Interchange (EDI) update', Westwood, MA: author.

Fayen, E.G. (1983), *The Online catalog: Improving Public Access to Library Materials*, White Plains, NY: Knowledge Industry Publications, Inc.

Fisher, R. and Ury, W. (1981), *Getting to YES: Negotiating Agreement Without Giving In*, Penguin.

Glicksman, M. (1984), 'The impact of computers on universities', in *Proceedings of the Ninth IBM–University Study Conference 1984*, Milford, CT: IBM Academic Information Systems, 19–28.

Glicksman, M. (1985), 'Supporting scholarship in universities: A response to the growing cost of information services', in P. Spyers-Duran and T.W. Mann, Jr. (eds.), *Financing Information Services*, Westport, CT: Greenwood Press, 49–68.

Glicksman, M. (1987), 'Computer technology and the three c's of higher education', in M. McGill (ed.), *Campus of the Future: Conference on Information Resources*, Dublin, OH: OCLC, 23–33.

Hand, W.B. (1988), 'Lease-for-hire: One way to find network personnel', *Data Communications*, September, 169–176.

'Hanover closes library in cost-cutting drive' (1988), *American Banker*, **153**(19), 14.

Hesse, B.W. and Grantham, C.E. (1991), 'Electronically distributed work communities: implications for research on telework', *Electronic Networking: Research, Applications, and Policy*, **1**, Fall, 4–17.

Lancaster, F.W. (1982), *Libraries and Librarians in an Age of Electronics*. Arlington, VA: Information Resources.

Lanham, R.A. (1990), 'Electronic texts and university structures', in *Scholarship and Research Libraries in the 21st Century*. Occasional paper no. 14. Washington, DC: American Council of Learned Societies.

Lanier, R.E. (1990), 'Knowledge management: Refining roles in scientific communication', *EDUCOM Review*, Fall, 21–27.

'Los Angeles County PL conducts $600,000 PR campaign' (1991), *Library Journal*, April 1, 19.

Lowry, C. (1990), 'Resource sharing or cost shifting? The unequal burden of cooperative cataloging and ILL in network', *College & Research Libraries*, **51**(1), 11–19.

Lyman, P. (1990), 'Non-commercial publishing', A presentation at the *Coalition for Networked Information Meeting*, Washington, DC, November 4.

Lyman, P., Gilbert, S. and Connolly, F. (1990), *Electronic Citizen's Bill of Rights*. Washington, DC: Office of Technology Assessment.

Matheson, N.W. and Cooper, A.D. (1982), 'Academic information in the academic health sciences center: Roles for the library in information management', *Journal of Medical Education, Part 2*, October.

Matthews, J.R. (1986), 'Growth and consolidation: The 1985 automated library system marketplace', *Library Journal*, April 1, 25–37.

Meyers, B. and Fleming, J. (1991), 'Price analysis and the serials situation: Trying to solve an age-old problem', *Journal of Academic Librarianship*, **17**(2), 86–92.

Mosco, V. (1989), *The Pay-Per Society: Computers and Communication in the Information Age: Essays in Critical Theory and Public Policy*. Norwood, NJ: Ablex.

Murdick, R.G., Bender, B. and Russell, R.S. (1990), *Service Operations Management*. Boston: Allyn and Bacon.

Naisbitt, J. and Aburdene, P. (1990), *Megatrends 2000*. New York, NY: Avon Books.

Nash, J. (1991), 'Companies try out "halfway" telecommuting', *Computerworld*, December 16, 73.

Norton, B. (1988), *Charging for Library and Information Services*. London: The Library Association.

Okerson, A. and Stubbs, K. (1991), 'The library "Doomsday Machine"', *Publishers Weekly*, February, 36–37.

O'Neill, G.K. (1981), *2081: A Hopeful View of the Human Future*. New York: Simon & Schuster.

Peters, P.E. (1991), 'Networked information resources and services: Next steps', *CAUSE/EFFECT*, **14**(2), 27–39.

Petersen, H.C. (1990), 'University libraries and pricing practices by publishers of scholarly journals', *Research in Higher Education*, **31**(4), 307–314.

'Photocopying chain found in violation of copyright law', (1991), *Chronicle of Higher Education*, April 3, A1.

Potter, W.G. (1986), 'Online catalogues in North America: An overview', *Automated Library and Information Systems (England)*, April, 120–130.

Quarterman, J.S (1990), *The Matrix*. Bedford, MA: Digital Press.

Reynolds, D. (1985), *Library Automation: Issues and Applications*. New York: Bowker.

Roberts, M.M. (1990), 'Packet accounting for network services', *EDUCOM Review*, **25**(3), 9–10.

Schiller, H.I. (1991), 'Public information goes corporate', *Library Journal*, October 1, 42–45.

Scully, J. and Byrne, J.A. (1987), *Odyssey: Pepsi to Apple . . . A Journey of Adventure, Ideas, and the Future*. Toronto: Fitzhenry and Whiteside.

Sirbu, Marvin (1991), *Development Plan for an Electronic Library System, Final Report*. Pittsburgh, PA: Information Networking Institute, Class of 1990, Carnegie Mellon University.

Stubbs, K. (1991), *ARL Statistics, 1989–1990*, Washington, DC: Association of Research Libraries.

Talaga, J. and Haley, J.W. (1991), 'Marketing theory applied to price discrimination in journals', *Journal of Academic Librarianship*, **16**(6), 348–351.

Taylor, R.S. (1984), 'Value-added processes in document-based systems: abstracting and indexing services', *Information Services and Use*, **4**, 127–146.

Council of Federal Libraries, *To Charge or Not to Charge: A Guide for Federal Libraries* (1981), Ottawa: Government of Canada.

'USC revamps its campus computer network' (1990), *Chronicle of Higher Education*, November 28, A22.

Viviano, R.P. (1984), 'Equipment leasing: a strategy for capital equipment acquisition', *Journal of Information & Image Management*, October, 32.

Walton, R. (1991), 'Shared automated systems governance: A checklist of issues', *Library Journal*, May 1, 66, 68.

Weber, R. (1991), 'Pricing, property and prospects: Electronic publishing in the 90s', Presentation at the *Coalition for Networked Information Conference on the Information Pricing Crisis*, Monterey, CA.

West, R.P. and Katz, R.N. (1990), 'Implementing the vision: A framework and agenda for investing in academic computing', *EDUCOM Review*, **25**(4), 32–27.

White, H.S. (1988), 'What price salami?: The federal process of contracting out libraries', *Library Journal*, January, 58–59.

Winkler, M. (1989), 'Not so full disclosure: SEC to quietly close reference rooms', *Money and Investing*, January 11, 1.

Woodsworth, A. (1991), *Patterns and Options for Managing Information Technology on Campus*, Chicago, IL: American Library Association.

Woodsworth, A., Allen, N., Hoadley, I., Lester, J., Molholt, P., Nitecki, D., and Wetherbee, L. (1989), 'The model research library: Planning for the future', *Journal of Academic Librarianship*, **15**, 132–138.

Woodsworth, A. and Williams, J.F. II (1988), 'Computer centers and libraries: In passage toward partnerships', *Library Administration and Management*, **2**, 85–90.

Index